D1134373

Luckenbooth

Luckenbooth

**an anthology
of
Edinburgh poetry**

edited by
Lizzie MacGregor
introduction by James Robertson

Polygon

in association with

SCOTTISH POETRY LIBRARY

By leaves we live

First published in 2007 by Polygon,
an imprint of Birlinn Limited

West Newington House
10 Newington Road
Edinburgh
EH9 1QS

www.birlinn.co.uk

Published in association with The Scottish Poetry Library
5 Crichton's Close, Edinburgh EH8 8DT
www.spl.org.uk

The publishers gratefully acknowledge the support of
The Binks Trust and the Russell Trust towards the publication of this volume

ISBN10: 1 84697 018 0
ISBN13: 978 1 84697 018 4

British Library Cataloguing-in-Publication Data
A catalogue record for this book is available from the British Library.

Design by Ann Ross Paterson
Printed and bound by Athenaeum Press, Gateshead

CONTENTS

INTRODUCTION

Edinburgh, as has often been noted, has inspired writers for many centuries. Not just poets, but novelists, essayists, journalists and travel writers have all had plenty to say about the city, some of it far from flattering. Tobias Smollett may have had one of his characters in *Humphry Clinker* (1771) declare, "Edinburgh is a hot-bed of genius", but 150 years later Lewis Grassic Gibbon was less complimentary, likening the capital to "a disappointed spinster, with a hare-lip and inhibitions". And what should we make of Patrick Geddes' outburst in a letter to R. B. Cunninghame Graham in 1909?

> Look with me at this sad old city – you see her pinioned by her judges and preyed on by their wig-lice, that countless vermin of lawyerlings, swollen and small. You see her left in squalor by her shopkeepers, the bawbee-worshipping bailie-bodies, and pushioned by her doctors; you hear her dulled by the blithers of her politicians and deived by the skreigh of the newsboy-caddies who squabble at their heels, and you know how she has been paralysed by the piffle of her professors . . . or driven into alternate hidebound or hysteric nightmares by every chilly dogmatism, every flaring hell-blast imagined by three centuries and more of diabologiac Divines.

The implication seems to be that poor Auld Reikie has been ill-served by its inhabitants through the ages. Even in that period of Enlightenment so succinctly summarised by Smollett, the place was as famous for its squalor as for its erudition. Yet we should be grateful for the candour of these various commentators. The most tedious aspect of Paradise, should such a place be attainable and should one attain it, would surely be the endless singing of hymns of stone-cold praise. Edinburgh, by contrast, is human and real, and, judging from the literary evidence, its history has been marked more by the foibles than the virtues of humankind.

But it is also, in the very manifestation of its reality, unreal. The city is laid out – draped, clustered, piled – against an astonishing landscape: it is, in Robert Louis Stevenson's phrase, a "precipitous

9

city", and an uneasy, disconcerting relationship exists between the built and natural environment, a relationship that has an effect on all those who dwell or visit there, whether or not they recognise it. It is as if, in an atlas, a "physical" map were imperfectly overlaid with a "political" one covering the same territory. "The old town," Dorothy Wordsworth commented in her journal in 1803, "with its irregular houses, stage upon stage, seen as we saw it, in the obscurity of a rainy day, hardly seems the work of men, it is more like a piling up of rocks". Thus the wider, wilder world has an uncanny ability to intrude into the minutiae of everyday urban life.

Stevenson, who knew the mysteries and mundanities of Edinburgh as well as anyone, captured this in a wonderful series of sketches, his *Picturesque Notes* of 1878–9. "You peep under an arch, you descend stairs that look as if they would land you in a cellar, you turn to the back-window of a grimy tenement in a lane: – and behold! you are face-to-face with distant and bright prospects. You turn a corner, and there is the sun going down into the Highland hills. You look down an alley, and see ships tacking for the Baltic."

This is a characteristic that the late Enric Miralles, the Catalan architect of the new Scottish Parliament, recognised and sought to exploit in his design of the building: the city intersects and interacts with the land (and, indeed, with the sea), and the modern political heart of Scotland had somehow to reflect that. Miralles was undoubtedly a perceptive observer, but he was also only the latest in a string of witnesses to the almost magical qualities of light, texture, shape, gradient and perspective that Edinburgh possesses in abundance.

No surprise, then, that fantasy and metaphor are co-opted in this anthology to produce images of Edinburgh in various surreal guises, as, for example, the enchanted ship of Lewis Spence's "The Prows o' Reekie", or as the scene for hopscotch-playing Lords of Session in John Oliver's "Peevers in Parliament Square". But there is always another viewing angle, the one that undercuts such fantasising before it gets carried away with itself, the down-to-earth face – or volte-face – that in Christine De Luca's words makes Edinburgh "the big sister of all cities, / forever tut-tutting".

It is clear from the oldest poem in this book that very little has changed for a very long time. William Dunbar, who was perfectly capable of the rich, surreal vein when he turned his mind to it, tut-tuts splendidly in his address "To the Merchantis of Edinburgh", and yet his poem revels in the very things he is objecting to:

> May nane pas throw your principall gaittis,
> For stink of haddockis and of scattis,
> For cryis of carlingis and debaittis,
> For feusum flyttingis of defame.
>   Think ye not schame,
> Befoir strangeris of all estaittis,
> That sic dishonour hurt your name?

Since Dunbar, almost every poet who has taken Edinburgh to his or her heart, from Robert Fergusson to Norman MacCaig to Valerie Gillies, has followed his cue, gleefully recording the shoulder-rubbing of duchess and drunkard, beggar and bourgeois, solicitor and strumpet, which takes place, or may at any moment take place, on every street-corner and at every close-mouth in the city. Edinburgh may have sprawled far beyond its original narrow bounds, yet somehow the confrontations and contradictions of the centre radiate out to the schemes and suburbs miles away.

The energy generated by these contrasts fuels much of the verse in *Luckenbooth*. There is no reason to suspect that, in fifty or a hundred years' time, another anthology will not tap into that same source and produce a further wave of poetry, new, yet also connected to these and earlier voices. Tradition for tradition's sake can have a deadening effect on any art form: tradition that opens itself to the future, that sets precedents rather than parameters, is invigorating. And there is plenty in these pages to inspire fresh words about, and a fresh look at, the city of Edinburgh.

James Robertson
August 2007

EDITOR'S NOTE

I came to live in Edinburgh in the early 1970s and I am still in love with the city – it constantly delights me. Edinburgh has inspired a great wealth of poems; I am very pleased to have had the opportunity to gather a number of them together into this collection and give something back to the city that has made me welcome.

Any collection of writing about Edinburgh cannot help but emphasise what a singular place it is, shaped by the astonishing landscape born of geological violence, then by the turmoil of its history and the often opposing forces of education and religion. We who live here bear the burden of an amazing legacy. A city must change in order to stay alive; this collection is testimony to those changes, but also to Edinburgh's essential spirit.

I hope that those who read it, including all the latter-day "merchantis of renoun" whose buildings, plans and strategies shape the city, will take to heart the import of the unique heritage we must not squander.

I would like to thank Robyn Marsack at the Scottish Poetry Library for her support; Lilias Fraser for her patience; the staff at Polygon; and above all my husband, family and friends for their forbearance while I have been busy with this book.

L.M.

Looking at Edinburgh

Far set in fields and woods, the town I see
Spring gallant from the shallows of her smoke …

Robert Louis Stevenson
from SONGS OF TRAVEL XXXVI

from SONGS OF TRAVEL XXXVI

The tropics vanish, and meseems that I,
From Halkerside, from topmost Allermuir
Or steep Caerketton, dreaming gaze again
Far set in fields and woods, the town I see
Spring gallant from the shallows of her smoke,
Cragged, spired, and turreted, her virgin fort
Beflagged. About, on seaward-drooping hills,
New folds of city glitter. Last, the Forth
Wheels ample waters set with sacred isles,
And populous Fife smokes with a score of towns.

Robert Louis Stevenson

IN PENTLAND WINE

Up here with the wind in our faces,
    And the brown heath under our feet,
We look through the shimmering spaces
    Over tower and steeple and street
To the Lion splendidly sleeping,
    To the tall Crags silent and grey,
To the Castle its grim guard keeping,
    And the shining shield of the Bay.

Behind us the mists of the valley
    Lie low on the moorland's breast,
With the bonnie banks of Bonaly
    In the grey of the winter dressed.
The west wind, wanton, is chiding
    Glencorse with the scourge of his whips,
And the wild ducks over it riding
    Are tossed like storm-tossed ships.

Up here with the clean winds blowing,
    I look to you, City of mine,
I fill me a goblet o'erflowing
    And pledge you in Pentland wine!
With a full heart thrilled by your story,
    While the hills stand round like kings,
I drink to your lasting glory
    In the wine that the hill-wind brings!

Will H. Ogilvie

EDINBURGH VOLTE-FACE

City of seven hills
rivalling Rome: you are
the big sister of all cities,
forever tut-tutting.

City of venerable skylines;
each morning you un-do yourself
like someone more anxious to save the wrapping
than enjoy the gift.

City of open spaces: for you
no strollers in the forum; merely
a scurry of solicitors, vellum-faced
with long north-facing days,
and little women, worn
from cleaning other people's stairs.

City of the great estates;
you have no outer wall, but numerous apartheids
charitably maintained.

City of seven hills
rivalling Rome: I hold your negative
to the light, and see
your true topography.

Christine De Luca

from MARMION, Canto IV

Still on the spot Lord Marmion stay'd,
For fairer scene he ne'er survey'd.
  When sated with the martial show
  That peopled all the plain below,
  The wandering eye could o'er it go,
  And mark the distant city glow
    With gloomy splendour red;
  For on the smoke-wreaths, huge and slow,
  That round her sable turrets flow,
    The morning beams were shed,
  And ting'd them with a lustre proud,
  Like that which streaks a thunder-cloud.
Such dusky grandeur cloth'd the height,
Where the huge Castle holds its state,
  And all the steep slope down,
Whose ridgy back heaves to the sky,
Pil'd deep and massy, close and high,
  Mine own romantic town!

Sir Walter Scott

EDINBURGH

A windy toon o cloods an' sunny glints;
  pinnacled, turreted, stey an' steep grey toon;
her soughin' gables sing their norlan' rants
  tae saut an' caller blufferts on her croon.

Steeple an' toor an' battlement stand bauld,
  an' gaze ootowre the kindly lands o Forth
tae the braid seaward lift, far, clear an' cauld,
  an' front her airt, the stern, abidin' north.

Oh, I hae seen her leamin' frae afar,
  bricht thro the fleetin' blatter o the rain,
an' happed an' hidden, rowed in norsea haar,
  secret an' dour, loom grandly, prood an' lane.

Tae stand an' watch frae oot the wooded west
  the heich ranks o her dignity gang by,
an' see it surgein' seaward, crest on crest,
  her lang swell merchan' ridged against the sky.

George Campbell Hay

soughin'	*sighing*
norlan' rants	*northern songs*
saut an' caller blufferts	*salty, bracing blasts*
lift	*sky*
airt	*direction*
leamin'	*gleaming*
rowed	*swathed*
norsea haar	*North Sea mist*

EDINBURGH

Midnight

Glasgow is null,
Its suburbs shadows
And the Clyde a cloud.

Dundee is dust
And Aberdeen a shell.

But Edinburgh is a mad god's dream,
Fitful and dark,
Unseizable in Leith
And wildered by the Forth,
But irresistibly at last
Cleaving to sombre heights
Of passionate imagining
Till stonily,
From soaring battlements,
Earth eyes Eternity.

Hugh MacDiarmid

THE EDINBURGH POEM

Here, where

we boast seven hills like Rome
(and even another three)

and upturned boats are the metaphor
to enshrine new Scotland's destiny,

our toast is "Wha's like us!" …
as if anyone else would want to be?

Here, where

glaciers and volcanoes shaped
the slopes of our geology

and a devoted dog is more celebrated
than those who fought for liberty,

no one could mistake
the tedium of travel for the odyssey.

Here, where

the surcharge is our presumption
and only the wind from the Forth is free

and the rich lodge, as ever,
in the same close with poverty,

if you live outwith our city,
such misfortune gets no sympathy.

Here, where

the tolbooth's gone with the gallows tree
yet we still spit on their memory

and our national monument endures
unfinished (by thrift or lethargy?),

you must allow some hazard
in the ambition of our democracy.

Here, where

our traditional litter
grows more generous by the year

and there's tartan with the pizza
or haggis with the brie,

it takes less than an hour
to escape to Glasgow or Kirkcaldy.

Gael Turnbull

Note: This is one possible setting of a kinetic poem, constructed for "busking", with
option of some audience interaction, and first presented at the Edinburgh Festival
Fringe Sunday, in the Meadows, 2001.

THE CITY WE LIVE IN

You are on my skyline
as high as eye is lifted
nothing is beyond you.

I approach and
come up against
walls
your rock defences.

You bridge my extremes
lead over, across
between one level and another.

I pass within the shadow
of your arches
and walk the colonnade.

Crescent and high terrace
would not entice me but
for sudden vista:

statue, campanile,
pearl of sea, jade of hill
well-proportioned temple.

More than these
I try the narrow steps
tunnelled wynds, wrought-iron gates

that lead me where
an inner court
holds itself secluded.

Tessa Ransford

THE PROWS O' REEKIE

O wad this braw hie-heapit toun
Sail aff like an enchanted ship,
Drift owre the warld's seas up and doun,
And kiss wi' Venice lip to lip,
Or anchor into Naples' Bay
A misty island far astray
Or set her rock to Athens' wa',
Pillar to pillar, stane to stane,
The cruikit spell o' her backbane,
Yon shadow-mile o' spire and vane,
Wad ding them a', wad ding them a'!
Cadiz wad tine the admiralty
O' yonder emerod fair sea,
Gibraltar frown for frown exchange
Wi' Nigel's crags at elbuck-range,
The rose-red banks o' Lisbon make
Mair room in Tagus for her sake.

A hoose is but a puppet-box
To keep life's images frae knocks,
But mannikins scrieve oot their sauls
Upon its craw-steps and its walls;
Whaur hae they writ them mair sublime
Than on yon gable-ends o' time?

Lewis Spence

ding them a'	beat them all
tine	lose
elbuck	elbow
scrieve	write
craw-steps	stepped gable of a roof

History

Oh ay, it was grand and glorious,
Splendant wi banners and nobilitie
– Nae greater granderie ere was
Than was kent by thae grey stanes ...

Sydney Goodsir Smith
from KYND KITTOCK'S LAND

OLD EDINBURGH

Down the Canongate
down the Cowgate
go vermilion dreams
snake's tongues of bannerets
trumpets with words from their mouths
saying *Praise me, praise me.*

Up the Canongate
up the Cowgate
lice on the march
tar on the amputated stump
Hell speaking with the tongue of Heaven
a woman tied to the tail of a cart.

And history leans by a dark entry
with words from his mouth
that say *Pity me, pity me*
but never forgive.

Norman MacCaig

from TO THE MERCHANTIS OF EDINBURGH

Quhy will ye, merchantis of renoun,
Lat Edinburgh, your nobill toun,
For laik of reformatioun
The commone proffeitt tyine, and fame?
    Think ye not schame,
That onie uther regioun,
Sall with dishonour hurt your name?

May nane pas throw your principall gaittis,
For stink of haddockis and of scattis,
For cryis of carlingis and debaittis,
For feusum flyttingis of defame.
    Think ye not schame,
Befoir strangeris of all estaittis,
That sic dishonour hurt your name?

Your Stinkand Stull, that standis dirk,
Haldis the lycht fra your parroche kirk;
Your foirstairis makis your housis mirk,
Lyk na cuntray bot heir at hame.
    Think ye not schame,
Sa litill polesie to work,
In hurt and sklander of your name? …

Your burgh of beggeris is ane nest,
To schout thai swentyouris will not rest,
All honest folk they do molest,
Sa piteuslie thai cry and rame.
    Think ye not schame,
That for the poore hes nothing drest,
In hurt and sclander of your name?

Your proffeit daylie dois incres,
Your godlie workis les and les.
Through streittis nane may mak progres,
For cry of cruikit, blind and lame.
    Think ye not schame,
That ye sic substance dois posses,
And will nocht win ane bettir name?

Sen for the Court and the Sessioun,
The great repair of this regioun
Is in your burgh, thairfoir be boun
To mend all faultis that ar to blame,
    And eschew schame.
Gif thai pas to ane uther toun,
Ye will decay, and your great name.

William Dunbar

tyine	*lose*
carlingis	*old women*
feusum flyttingis	*foul squabbles*
Stinkand Stull	*alley through the Luckenbooths*
parroche kirk	*St Giles*
swentyouris	*scoundrels*
rame	*clamour*
sen	*since*

NA FAOILEAGAN MAIDNE

Siud a dhùisg mi moch air mhadainn,
gàir fhaoileagan os cionn an taighe,
's iad air tighinn bhàrr na mara.

A' goir: "Dhùn Èideann! Dhùn Èideann!
tha gile sear a' dìreadh speuraibh
air chionn èirigh na grèine;
tha dol air ais air na reultan;
tha driùchd air craobhan 's air feur ann,
tha driùchd air craoibh, air flùr, air feur ann.
Tha solais shràid 'fàs fann, is èistear
ceud fhuaim na trafaig 'dol nas dèine.
Tha daoin' a' dùsgadh roimhn èirigh.
An cuimhne leò an t-àm a thrèig sinn
's an robh rìghrean an Dùn Èideann,
's cùirtearan air am beulaibh;
teachdairean à tìrean cèine;
clàrsach is cruit air ghleus ann;
fìon ga òl is ceòl ga èisteachd?"

A' goir: "Dhùn Èideann! Dhùn Èideann!"

Deòrsa Mac Iain Dheòrsa

THE MORNING GULLS

It was that which woke me early in the morning,
the cry of seagulls above the house.
They had come from the sea.

Crying: "Edinburgh! Edinburgh!
There is a whiteness in the east climbing the sky
before the rising of the sun.
The stars are fading.
There is dew on trees and grass;
there is dew on tree, on flower, on grass.
The street lights grow faint, and there can be heard
the first noise of the traffic growing in intensity.
People are waking and thinking of rising.
Do they remember the time that has forsaken us,
when there were kings in Edinburgh
and courtiers in their presence;
ambassadors from far-off lands;
great harp and little harp in tune there;
drinking of wine and listening to music?"

Crying: "Edinburgh! Edinburgh!"

George Campbell Hay

from AULD REIKIE

Now morn, with bonny purpie-smiles,
Kisses the air-cock o' St Giles;
Rakin their een, the servant lasses
Early begin their lies and clashes;
Ilk tells her friend o' saddest distress,
That still she brooks frae scouling mistress;
And wi her joe in turnpike stair
She'd rather snuff the stinking air,
As be subjected to her tongue,
When justly censur'd in the wrong.

On stair wi tub, or pat in hand,
The barefoot housemaids loo to stand,
That antrin fock may ken how snell
Auld Reikie will at morning smell:
Then, with an inundation big as
The burn that 'neath the Nore Loch Brig is,
They kindly shower Edina's roses,
To quicken and regale our noses.
Now some for this, wi satire's leesh,
Hae gien auld Edinburgh a creesh:
But without souring nocht is sweet;
The morning smells that hail our street
Prepare, and gently lead the way
To simmer canty, braw and gay;
Edina's sons mair eithly share
Her spices and her dainties rare,
Than he that's never yet been call'd
Aff frae his plaidie or his fauld.

Now stairhead critics, senseless fools,
Censure their aim, and pride their rules,
In Luckenbooths, wi glowring eye,
Their neighbour's sma'est faults descry:
If ony loun should dander there,
Of aukward gate and foreign air,
They trace his steps, till they can tell
His pedigree as weel's himsel.

Robert Fergusson

purpie-smiles	*blushes*
antrin fock	*other people*
snell	*keen*
Edina's roses	*contents of the chamber pots*
creesh	*thrashing*
canty	*pleasant*
eithly	*easily*
Luckenbooths	*buildings housing shops, on the north side of St Giles*
loun	*fellow*
dander	*wander*

ANNALS OF ENLIGHTENMENT

Hume passes
into the absolute,
brace-girdled, without
concern.

      James,
laird of Auchinleck,
as this transpires, lays
boisterous breath along
his doxy's shoulder,

elevates the skirt,
and takes her on the dust
of a stonemason's table,
some way below the Castle hill.

*

In or out
of armour, which
would you rather –

cool release of the *bon philosophe*,
or Boswell's perturbation?

Much to be endured,
and little to be enjoyed?

or what mix in between?

*

At ten, a drum
for clart and creesh
on close and vennel.

The wind
in a shift lifts
leaves along old
Calton wall.

Alexander Hutchison

clart and creesh   *dirt and grease*
close and vennel   *passageway and alley*

The philosopher David Hume died a committed atheist; James Boswell was racked by Calvinist guilt over his promiscuity.

from EDINBURGH; OR, THE ANCIENT ROYALTY:
A SKETCH OF FORMER MANNERS

Then were the days of comfort and of glee!
When met to drink a *social cup of tea* –
The chequer'd chairs, in seemly circle placed;
The Indian tray, with Indian china graced;
The red stone Tea-pot with its silver spout;
The Tea Spoons numbered, and the tea *fill'd out!*
Rich Whigs and Cookies *smoke* upon the board,
The best that Keir the baxter can afford.
Hapless the wight, who, with a lavish sup,
Empties too soon the lilliputian cup!
Tho' patience fails, and tho' with thirst he burns,
All – all must wait till the last cup returns.
That cup returned, now see the hostess ply
The tea-pot, measuring with equal eye;
To all again at once she grants the boon,
Dispensing her gunpowder by platoon.
They chat of dress (as ladies will) and cards,
And fifty friends within three hundred yards –
Or now they listen, all in merry glee,
While "Nancy Dawson", "Sandie o'er the lee",
(Than foreign cadence surely sweeter far)
Ring on the jingling spinet or guitar.
The clogs are ready when the treat is o'er,
And many a blazing lanthorn leaves the door.

Alexander Boswell

Whigs   *fine wheaten tea-breads*
baxter   *baker*

LITANY OF TIME PAST

What's today?
　Hoops today.
What's yesterday?
　Tops yesterday.
What's tomorrow?
　Diabolo.

Moons and planets come out to play,
The Bear bowled, the Sun spun.
See the Devil-on-sticks run
Today, tomorrow, and yesterday.

What's Hope?
　Skipping rope.
What's Charity?
　Salty peppery.
What's Faith?
　Edinburgh, Leith,
　Portobello, Musselburgh,
　And Dalkeith.

Out you are.
　In you are.
Mustard.
　Vinegar.

Muriel Spark

bho ÒRAN DHÙN ÈIDEANN

'S e baile mòr Dhùn Èideann
   A b' èibhinn leam bhith ann,
Àite fialaidh farsaing
   A bha tlachdmhor anns gach ball;
Gearasdain is batraidh
   Is rampairean gu teann,
Taighean mòra 's caisteal
    Anns an tric an d' stad an camp.

'S tric a bha camp rìoghail ann,
   'S bu rìomhach an luchd-dreuchd,
Trùp nan srann-each lìonmhor
Gu dìleas air a' ghèard;
Bhiodh gach fear cho eòlach
   Sa h-uile seòl a b' fheàrr,
Na fleasgaich bu mhath fòghlam
   A dhol an òrdugh blàir.

'S iomadh fleasgach uasal ann
   A bha gu suairce grinn,
Fùdar air an gruagan
A suas gu bàrr an cinn;
Leadain dhonna dhualach
   'Na chuachagan air snìomh,
Bàrr dosach mar an sìoda
   Nuair shlìogadh e le cìr.

'S mòr a tha dc bhaintighearnan
   A-null 's a-nall an t-sràid,
Gùntaichean den t-sìoda orr'
Gan slìogadh ris a' bhlàr;
Staidhs air na h-ainnirean
   Gan teannachadh gu h-àrd,
Buill-mhais' air aodainn bhòidheach,
   Mar thuilleadh spòrsa dhaibh.

Donnchadh Bàn Mac an t-Saoir

from SONG OF EDINBURGH

'Tis in Edinburgh city
I would rejoice to be –
a bountiful and spacious place
that pleased in all respects:
garrison and battery
and ramparts all compact;
great buildings and a castle
where oft the camp has stayed.

Oft a royal camp was there,
and gorgeous were the officers;
a numerous troop of snorting horse
faithfully mounted guard;
every man was so expert
in all the best manoeuvres,
those lads who had good training
to deploy in battle order.

Many noble beaux are there,
urbane and elegant,
having powder on their wigs
right up to their crowns;
auburn, plaited tresses
twisted into curls;
and like silk is the bushy top,
when it is smoothed by comb.

Many patrician ladies
go up and down the street,
all wearing gowns of silk
that brush against the ground;
stays are worn by the damsels,
compressing them above,
with beauty spots on pretty faces,
to increase their coquetry.

Duncan Ban MacIntyre
(Translated by Angus MacLeod)

from EDINBURGH CRIES

Loud the cries are ringin', ringin',
   Cheery ringin' up an' doun;
Short but sweet the sang that's singin',
   Blithely through Auld Reekie's toun.
Wanderin' weary, wet or dry,
Hark yon sonsy maiden's cry –
"Four bunch a penny, the bonnie caller radishes!"
Oh they're bonnie! come an' see them!
Taste an' try before ye buy.

Ilka month brings in its treasures –
   Rizarts red, in clusters shine;
Bonnie berries, green an' yellow;
   Sugar-ploums sae sweet an' fine.
Wanderin' weary, wet or dry,
Hark yon sturdy hizzie's cry –
"Neeps like succar – wha'll buy neeps!"
Oh they're bonnie! come an' see them!
Taste an' try before ye buy.

"Ripe strawberries!" "Sonsy cherries!"
   Greet the ear at ilka turn.
"Buy my bonnie water-cresses,
   A' the road frae Loudon Burn!"
Wanderin' weary, wet or dry,
Hark yon wifie's cheery cry –
      "Curds an' whey!"
Oh they're bonnie! come an' see them!
Taste an' try before ye buy …

"Wastlin' herrin'! wastlin' herrin'!"
   Come an' buy – they'll please ye weel.
"Haddies – haddies – caller haddies!"
   Fresh an' loupin in the creel.
Wanderin' weary, wet or dry,
Hark yon Fisher Jenny's cry –
         "Caller ou'!"
Oh they're bonnie! come an' see them!
Taste an' try before ye buy.

James Smith

sonsy	buxom, comely
caller	fresh
rizarts	redcurrants
hizzie	housewife
neeps	turnips
succar	sugar
wastlin'	west-coast
haddies	haddocks
caller ou'	fresh oysters

A longer version of "Edinburgh Cries" was later set to music.

from IN EDINBURGH 1940

Now, O let lovers lie close near Cramond Brig
And the children gather the frail clams beside Hound Point,
Beside the little island with the wooden beacon.
O let the summer ripen the clustered rowans,
And the fronds of bracken curl over the Pentland Hills.
Though the May Island be blinded by war, let the fish
Run through the booms, and the Forth break to the sea.

Under the lion-crouching shadow of Arthur's Seat,
Let me walk by the ruined palace, in the vision of history.
Let me walk by the volcanic rock, basalt crowned with the Castle,
In Charlotte Square let me hear Sir Walter Scott droning,
Drivelling a dream of history, and let me meet Burns,
Outside the Tron Bar, drunk with disgust as much as whisky:

In time of war let me ask him the expected questions –
Ask whether his rocks have melted with the sun
This summer, and whether the tides have all gone dry
Along the Ayrshire coast. O let me observe his distaste
For my cigarettes and half-pint of beer, my snigger of sex.
O do not leave me alone with the ghosts of the past …

Here the boy Rimbaud paused, flying love and lust,
Unnoticed on his journey to the Abyssinian plains
And the thick dropsy of his tender leg. Here the other Knox
Surgeon and anatomist, saw the beauty of the young girl
Smothered by Burke and Hare. And here, O certainly,
God was the private property of a chosen few
Whose lives ran carefully and correctly to the grave.

This, deny it as I like, is still my city and these ghosts,
Sneer as I may, have helped to make me what I am.
A woman cried in labour and Simpson inhaled his vapour
Falling, anaesthetised, across the drawing-room table.
John Graham, laird of Claverhouse, did not have tears
For those he killed, nor did the silver bullet weep for him.
This city, bulwark of the east wind, formed me as I am.

Ruthven Todd

Old Town

Gang doun nou, come doun and I'll lead ye
Intil the hairt of Scotland's hairt …

Sydney Goodsir Smith
from KYND KITTOCK'S LAND

FROM A WINDOW IN PRINCES STREET

Above the Crags that fade and gloom
Starts the bare knee of Arthur's Seat;
Ridged high against the evening bloom,
The Old Town rises, street on street;
With lamps bejewelled, straight ahead,
Like rampired walls the houses lean,
All spired and domed and turreted,
Sheer to the valley's darkling green;
Ranged in mysterious disarray,
The Castle, menacing and austere,
Looms through the lingering last of day;
And in the silver dusk you hear,
Reverberated from crag and scar,
Bold bugles blowing points of war.

W. E. Henley

ON THE MEND

Two small boys
walk the length
of the Royal Mile
with a hammer.

You can hear them
tapping on the bins
and scaffolding,
mending the city.

Jayne Wilding

CLOSE NAMES

Fishmarket Close and Fleshmarket Close,
preserved down the centuries, still
strike a chord; like Old Tolbooth Wynd
and the long gone Luckenbooth stalls,
their silver hearts intertwined; while
Hammerman's Entry summons
the bellows' roar, ring of iron on iron;
and Dunbar's Close, Cromwell's
Ironsides billeted after battle.

Sugarhouse Close and Bakehouse Close
boast their own past and function –
not quite Dippermouth and Porterhouse,
conjuring up images of New Orleans
cutting contests and tailgate trombones,
but suggestive of a distinctive music
resounding in the Royal Mile
throughout Scotland's history,
theirs a ground bass of a different kind;

now jaunty, the banners streaming,
now plucking the heartstrings
like the Blues, in the realisation
of things lost, the end of an auld sang.
As with the Blues too, a lingering
undertow of loss and deprivation:
the start of a new age – yet the city's
division into haves and have-nots
never more discordant than today.

Stewart Conn

from THE LAST SPEECH AND DYING WORDS
OF THE CROSS OF EDINBURGH

Which was hang'd, drawn and quartered, on Monday the 15th March, 1756,
for the horrid Crime of being an Incumbrance to the Street.

I was built up in *Gothic* times,
And have stood sev'ral hundred reigns;
Sacred my mem'ry and my name,
For Kings and Queens I did proclaim.
I peace and war did oft declare,
And rous'd my country ev'ry where ;
Your ancestors around me walk'd,
Your kings and nobles 'side me talk'd;
And lads and lasses, with delight,
Set tryst with me to meet at night;
No tryster e're was at a loss,
For why, *I'll meet you at the cross.*
I country people did direct
Through all the city with respect,
Who missing me, will look as droll
As mariners without the pole.
On me great men have lost their lives,
And for a *Maiden* left their wives.
Low rogues likeways oft got a peg
With turnip, t--d, or rotten egg;
And when the mob did miss their butt,
I was bedaub'd like any slut.
With loyal men, on loyal days,
I dress'd myself in lovely bays,
And with sweet apples treat the crowd,
While they huzza'd around me loud.
    Professions many have I seen,
And never have disturbed been:
I've seen the *Tory* party slain,
And *Whigs* exulting o'er the plain;
I've seen again the *Tories* rise,
And with loud shouting pierce the skies,

Then mount the scale, and chace the *Whig*,
From *Pentland-hill* to *Bothwel-brig*.
I've seen the covenants by all sworn,
And likeways seen them burnt and torn.
I neutral stood, as peaceful *Quaker*,
With neither side was I partaker.

    I wish my life had longer been,
That I might greater ferlies seen;
Or else like other things decay,
Which Time alone doth waste away:
But since I now must lose my head,
I, at my last, this lesson read:
"Tho' wealth, and youth, and beauty shine,
And all the graces round you twine,
Think on your end, nor proud behave,
There's nothing sure this side the grave."

"Claudero"

Maiden   *guillotine*
ferlies   *marvels*

The present Mercat Cross, standing just east of St Giles, was assembled in 1885, incorporating parts of the original.

THE SEAT O' INSPIRATION

(Amang the Burns relics at Lady Stair's Hoose are twa stules used by the Poet
when correctin priefs at the printer's)

I rubbed my dowp on Rabbie's stule
When naebody was by,
Ae day at Lady Stair's braw Hoose;
Forgie me gin I craw owre croose
But, fegs, I hae a graun excuse –
Ye'll ken the reason why.

Rab had mair genius in his dowp,
I'd be prepared to bet,
Than a' the wits o' ilka schule
Could muster in a common pule.
I rubbed my dowp on Rabbie's stule –
I'll be a poet yet!

Douglas Fraser

dowp   backside
craw ower croose   boast

AT ROBERT FERGUSSON'S GRAVE
October 1962

Canongait kirkyaird in the failing year
is auld and grey, the wee roseirs are bare,
five gulls leam white agin the dirty air:
why are they here? There's naething for them here.

Why are we here oursels? We gaither near
the grave. Fergusons mainly, quite a fair
turn-out, respectfu, ill at ease, we stare
at daith – there's an address – I canna hear.

Aweill, we staund bareheidit in the haar,
murnin a man that gaed back til the pool
twa-hunner year afore our time. The glaur

that haps his banes glowres back. Strang, present dool
ruggs at my hairt. Lichtlie this gin ye daur:
here Robert Burns knelt and kissed the mool.

Robert Garioch

roseirs	*rose bushes*
leam	*gleam*
haar	*mist*
glaur	*mud*
dool	*sorrow*
ruggs	*tugs*
lichtlie	*belittle*
gin ye daur	*if you dare*
mool	*earth on a grave*

PEEVERS IN PARLIAMENT SQUARE

(Suggested by seeing a large and beautifully executed Peever-Court chalked out in the
centre of Parliament Square. March 1954.)

They're playin' at Peevers in Parliament Square,
In Parliament Square, in Parliament Square;
And judges and pleaders and writers are there,
    A' ettlin' to play at the Peevers.

They run oot like stour when they're by wi' their trokes,
To the beds, chalkit oot like a muckle square box
Atween Chairlie's horse and the grave o' John Knox –
    A gran' place to play at the Peevers!

The Lord President's sel', when the pleaders are mute
And he'd fain hae a change frae forensic dispute,
Has challenged the Lord Justice Clerk to come oot
    To see wha'll be best at the Peevers.

And the Writers and Advocates, gethert aroun,
They a' held their braiths and nane daurt mak' a soun,
As ilk ane cam forrit and kiltit his goun,
    Syne yerkit awa at the Peevers.

They stood on ae leg wi' nae shoogle or swither,
And the Peevers they skiffed frae ae square to anither,
And the hale Bench and Bar were sune roarin' thegither
    To see them sae gleg at the Peevers.

But the Lord Justice Clerk, he was soople and strang,
And it seemed he juist couldna dae onything wrang;
But the President *could* – and it wasna that lang
    Till he awned himsel bate at the Peevers.

And the Lord Justice Clerk said, "In maitters o' Law,
My Lord, there are nane that come near ye ava;
In fact, ye're the flooer o' the Parliament Ha',
    But ye're no worth a dawm at the Peevers."

But that nicht, when the mirk happit Parliament Ha',
And Pleaders and Writers had a' gane awa,
The mune lookit doon, and a ferlie she saw
    At the place where they'd played at the Peevers.

For she saw a dark shape that gaed slinkin' aboot
Aroun' Parliament Square wi' a pail and a cloot;
And syne it bent doon, and it clean wipit oot
    The beds where they'd played at the Peevers.

So the bonnie white beds noo are a' wede awa:
They're clean dichtit oot ayont hope o' reca',
And there's sighin' and sabbin' in Parliament Ha';
    For they canna get playin' at the Peevers.

John W. Oliver

peevers	*hopscotch*
ettlin'	*eager*
stour	*puff of dust*
trokes	*negotiations*
kiltit	*tucked up*
yerkit awa	*worked keenly*
shoogle or swither	*wobble or dither*
skiffed	*skimmed*
gleg	*nimble*
happit	*swathed*
ferlie	*strange sight*
cloot	*cloth*
dichtit	*wiped*

COUGAIT REVISITED

"Aa ony o us ever wantit was a hoose in Jeffrey Street"
– *Old lady, reminiscing on her life in the Cougait.*

Moving among sic stanes, I ken
I canna bide lang. I dinna mind
a time I wasna scunnered by this street
and I downa. Gin I could meet it
with a steady gaze for mair nor twa
three minutes at a time, I'd be gaffer
of that gang that's cawin it doun,
full of speiring wonder and a cowking disgust.

But I have no speiring now, no arguments,
no wonder. I hang about
thae black auld lands and dander owre
thae clairty gutters;
take a measure, make a count
of all the sinners, saints and ghaists
that dern ahint the snibbed and lockit shutters
time put up. And history for me
bides in nae dark entry, but maun forever
dree its kenless weird in the bonnier slums
of Burdiehouse, Gilmerton or even
a heich top-flat in the Dumbiedykes.

For hardly a soul of us ever won to Jeffrey Street.

Donald Campbell

scunnered	*disgusted*
downa	*dare not*
cawin	*pulling*
speiring	*questioning*
cowking	*retching*
dander	*wander*
clairty	*mucky*
dern	*hide*
dree	*endure*
kenless weird	*unknown fate*

THE VISION OF ENRIC MIRALLES (1)

A subtle game of views and implications
is what I play. Once, Edinburgh was this:
a mountain and some buildings, synthesis
of human and geological formations.
What we create must fit with what's on hand –
cut through the Old Town's grain and yet enhance,
be mindful of the past, and yet advance –
a Parliament that sits within the land,
a gathering where land and people meet.
The land itself will be a building-block:
to me this is of greatest consequence.
The Parliament will grow from Arthur's Seat,
a bridge between the city and the rock,
a mirror of the land it represents.

James Robertson

Enric Miralles was the Catalan architect whose design won the competition for the new Scottish Parliament building at Holyrood.

Hills of Edinburgh

I see Edinburgh sprawling like seven cats
on its seven hills beside the Firth of Forth.

Norman MacCaig
from ASSYNT AND EDINBURGH

ARTHUR'S SEAT

To lie ablow the ruits o a muckle ben
        And wait for a horn to blaw
And raise ye heich wi the strength o a hunder men
        For dingan the Deil awa
        – Nae dout thon's braw.

But lyin lane in a sleep yearhunders lang
        Wi only a cauldrife dwaum
O' a connached court, a queen whas rule was wrang,
        A country run ramstam
        – The thocht maun damn.

Poor hero-king! Sleep quate, sleep widdreme-free
        In deeps o the howie hill,
Leave time-and-tide til tinkers' getts like me
        And bide a byword still
        – For guid or ill.

Alexander Scott

ablow	*below*
dingan	*beating*
cauldrife dwaum	*chilly dream*
connached	*ruined*
ramstam	*uncontrolled*
widdreme	*nightmare*
howie	*hollow*
getts	*bastards*

Legend has it that Arthur of Britain lies sleeping beneath the hill.

FROM ARTHUR'S SEAT

North-east the Firth, a bracelet
merging with mist; south-west
the Pentlands, sharply defined. Directly
opposite, the castle. A sudden gust
makes me lose my footing. Gulls slip past,
eyeing us disdainfully.
On lower ground, we find respite.

Strange to contemplate this spot,
gouged cleanly out,
as going back millions of years;
its saucer fire and ice, volcanic
rock shaped by glaciers,
where now cameras click
and lovers stroll in pairs.

Such thoughts cannot be further
from the minds of those golfers
on the fairway below, heads down
and eyes on the ball, oblivious
to the shadows
furtively closing in,
the imminence of rain.

Tempting, watching us
loll here, to deduce
the same; whereas
it is often when happiest,
we are most conscious
of darkness. See, it sweeps
towards us, the rim of an eclipse.

Stewart Conn

DUMB SHOW, WITH CANDLES
from CAMERA OBSCURA

Still as a battlefield, the strewn city
goes under, slips into silhouette.
Some threads of smoke,
the lift and fall of flags in orange light.
The glinting windows go out one by one.

Low over the Firth, a fork of geese
comes pulling past, straight-necked:
creaking like rowlocks
over the frozen hill.
On the Parthenon below, querulous gulls
screel and skraik and peel away,
bickering, into the air's tow.
Too cold, even for them.
I circle the observatory one more time:
mine the only footprints in the snow.

Now the night has fallen, Edinburgh comes alight
as if each building's shell
has a fire inside that burned. The follies
– lit exhibits – stand here on the hill
in their white stone; the Castle glows.
And the streets are bright blurs of sodium
and pearl: the drawn tracery of headlamps
smeared in long exposure. For miles west
the city stretches,
laid with vapour trails and ghosts.

To the east, the folding sea has drowned
the girning of the gulls. A lighthouse
perforates the night: a slow cigarette.
Then there is no more light,
and no more breath or sound.

Robin Robertson

from THE WEE RAGGIT LADDIE TO THE LAIRD OF BLACKFORD HILL

Stout Laird o' Blackford Hill, let me
But gain your honour's lug a wee,
I fain wad let your lairdship see
                Sufficient cause
To mak your hill to a' as free
                    As ance it was.

Weel mind I o' the joyous days
I gathered hips, an' haws, an' slaes,
Climbing ower Blackford's heathy braes
                Birds' nests to herry,
Or smearing face, an' hands, an' claes,
                  Wi' bramble berry …

Then shall a laird whase kindly heart
Has ever ta'en the puir man's part,
Be reckon'd like some mean upstart,
                O' saulless stature,
Wha sells, as at an auction mart,
                  The face o' nature?

Though bairns may pu', when yap or drouthy,
A neep or bean, to taste their mouthy,
Losh, man! their hames are no sae couthy
                As your bien Ha';
Though puir folks' bairns are unco toothie,
                  Their feeding's sma'.

An' a' the neeps, an' a' the beans,
The hips, the haws, the slaes, the geens,
That e'er were pu'ed by hungry weans,
                Could ne'er be missed
By lairds like you, wi' ample means
                  In bank and kist.

Then listen to my earnest prayer,
An' open Blackford Hill ance mair;
Let us a' pree the caller air
                    That sweeps its braes,
An' mak it worth the poet's care
                    To sing your praise.

James Ballantine

yap or drouthy	hungry or thirsty
bien Ha'	comfortable house
geens	wild cherries
pree	taste
caller	fresh

Blackford Hill was bought for the people of Edinburgh in 1884 after a campaign by Provost Harrison.

THE GRAY ETIN

Ae dawin, frae Corstorphine lea
I saw a ferlie ill to dree,
The dragon-beast Auld Reekie streitch
Her hale lee-length and rax and reach
To drink her mornin' frae the sea.
She loupt; her skail o' sclates gleamed siller,
Then hirpled doun, the auld man-killer,
To sook the blae bree brimmed wi' faem
That ilka forenicht owre her kaim
She blaws in mist like amethyst,
That belchin' haar frae oot her wame
That fills fu' mony a coffin-kist.
As I on rigg cowered couthy there
Amazed, yon hills o' my despair
Heaved, and the veinings on her flanks
Were streets, her warts were kirks and banks,
Her teeth were pillars and her een
The Castel winnocks flashing sheen.
Then, like the Momnon o' the Nile,
Whilk gloamin' livens for a while,
Sank back to stane, and men, like louses,
Swarmed frae her tenements and hooses.
I thocht: "Aye, ye hae wale o' sauls;
Sae has a kebbuck; can the brawls
That mak a day upon your hurdies
Be ither than an hour o' Tophet?
Ye've a wale o' weevils and o' wordies,
But when did maggots need a prophet?"

Lewis Spence

ferlie	*wonder*
dree	*endure*
hirple	*hobble*
blae bree	*blue water*
kaim	*ridge*
haar	*mist*
rigg	*field*
winnocks	*windows*
wale	*choice*
kebbuck	*cheese*
hurdies	*flanks*

NORTHSONG

And if the haar crawls slowly up from Leith,
Chilling the flesh and bone, the flanks and teeth,
And if the wind turns east in the afternoon
To mock the calendar that points to June,
And if the sky is hard as lead or coal
And streets are tombs that have no sound or soul,
And if the faces of the young and old
Are grey and sad and tired and lost and cold –

I'll wave the sour and moaning heart away,
For in my head I nurse a magic day
When once I walked upon the Blackford Hill
In sun, after a week of rain and chill;
For at my feet there lay nine shades of green
That kings and southern eyes have never seen.

Stuart MacGregor

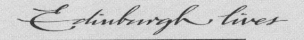

A city forms the folk conceived there ...

Alan Bold
from EDINBURGH

from ANGEL OF MORNINGSIDE

Well, em not one to complain – thet's not meh hebit –
But, eh tell you, Christian Aid Week's left me ebsolutely webbit.
Eh hed stood for hours collecting ootside Jenners,
Expecting to gether in a wheen o' tenners
End urging on every pesserbeh eh met
The immediate cencellation of all Third World foreign debt.

Well, ay good hef million people pessed me beh –
Not one of them looked me squarely in the eh.

Edded to which, it seems eh was no metch
For the professional competition on meh petch:
In front of M&S, ay raither naice old men
Selling the *War Creh* for the Selly Enn;
On aither side of him, of various genders,
En ebsolute betellion of *Big Issue* vendors;

End, gayzumping me, beneath a flennel rug,
Ay henna-rinsed Mohican with ay scebby dug,

Who produced a penny whistle oot o' his bedding
End proceeded to give us reams of *Mheri's Wedding*.
In the face of such concerted opposition
Eh felt eh hed to reconsider meh position
End the very ground on which meh faith is premised –
So eh moved fairther along, to Boots the Chemist.

Norman Bissett

webbit   *exhausted*

EDINBURGH

If they should ask what makes the stuff of us
   We should call up such idle things and gone!
The theatre we knew in Grindlay Street,
   The midnight bell vibrating in the Tron;

A church tower's clock along the Lothian Road
   Whose face lit up would turn a lemon moon,
Seen o'er the pallid bleakness of the street
   In the chill dusks that harry northern June,

A Sunday morning over Samson's Ribs,
   The smoky grass that grows on Arthur's Seat;
Turned-yellow willow leaves in Dalkeith Road,
   Dropt lanceheads on the pavement at our feet;

Glimpses got sometimes of the Forfar hills
   With the white snows upon them or, maybe,
Green waters washing round the piers of Leith
   With all the straws and flotsam of the sea.

A certain railway bridge whence one can look
   On a network of bright lines and feel the stress,
Tossing its plumes of milky snow, where goes
   Loud in full pace the thundering North Express

Behind its great green engine; or in Spring
    Black-heaved the Castle Rock and there where blows
By Gordon's window wild the wallflower still,
    The gold that keeps the footprints of Montrose.

The Pentlands over yellow stubble fields
    Seen out beyond Craigmillar; and the flight
Of seagulls wheeling round the dark-shared plough,
    Strewing the landscape with a rush of white.

Such idle things! Gold birches by hill lochs,
    The gales that beat the Lothian shores in strife,
The day you found the great blue alkanette,
    And all the farmlands by the shores of Fife.

Margot Robert Adamson

GÀRRADH MORAY PLACE, AN DÙN EIDEANN

Duilleagan dubha air an fheur,
fàileadh searbh na cloiche taise,
sop odhar de cheò
ga ìsleachadh mu na craobhan;
a' coimhead a-mach à bròn,
mòr-shùilean m' athar,
duilleag a' snìomh gu làr –
gluasad m' aigne.

Mun cuairt, coire thaighean drùidhteach,
comharra aois glòir-mhiannaich,
òrduighean cholbh clasaigeach
nach aithnich laigse san duine.

Gàrradh tathaichte aig bantraichean
fàilligeach, neo-eisimeileach,
a' coiseachd ann an cianalas an làithean,
an uallaichean ceilte.

Ach cluinnear an seo gliongartaich
coilearan chon grinn-cheumnach,
is chithear, fa chomhair nan taighean,
meanbh-dhuilleagan soilleir
gan leigeil sìos gu sèimh
aig a' bheithe chiùin, chuimir.

Meg Bateman

MORAY PLACE GARDENS, EDINBURGH

Black leaves on the grass,
an acrid smell of damp stonework,
a wisp of ochre fog
lowering itself around the trees;
looking out from sorrow,
my father's great eyes,
a leaf spinning to the ground –
the motion of my spirits.

All round, a cauldron of imposing houses,
sign of an ambitious age,
orders of classical columns
that do not countenance human frailty.

Gardens haunted by widows,
failing, independent,
walking in the wearisomeness of their days
their burdens concealed.

But tinkling is heard here
from the collars of the neat-stepping dogs,
and against the houses
tiny bright leaves are seen,
with the shapely birch tree
gently letting them go.

Meg Bateman

THE BIG SCHOOL

It grows from one of Edinburgh's seven hills:
This pagan temple on its jutty shelf
Extends its railway-blackened verticals,
Severe and chaste as Pallas is herself.
Yet fluted pillars, sheer retaining walls,

Their sweet Euclidian geometry,
Charm the barbarian granite of the cliff
Into a kind of Scots urbanity,
Inviolate (there's no front door) as if
Cold classicism likes humanity

A little at arm's length. And cold we are:
In winter (memory denominates
At least eleven months of winter there)
Not scarves, gloves, scalding pipes or spitting grates
Can purge the impatient crispness from the air.

Let Rectors bleat, through practised, public lips,
Of character and commonwealth, we know
Winning, of rugby games or scholarships,
Is solid pudding, and we make it so,
Elitist to our frozen fingertips.

John Whitworth

EDINBURGH SUBURB

Striding along your wide paved elegance
I wear no tights and one shoe flaps unbuckled.

I cast an appraising eye
at your privet hedges and pink and white cherry trees
now bent with blossom.

I arrived via my comprehensive education
and damp fairy tale cottages
built into damper embankments.

Once my princesses lived here.
They wore pale blue party dresses, buckled shoes
and silver christening bracelets.

Angela McSeveney

BETRAYAL IN MORNINSIDE

Embro my ain, ye are aye meant
tae be a city o middle-class douceness
                        blue-nosed mediocrity
                        bourgeois obtuseness

but
        (listen tae what I'm tellin ye!)
                        The ither nicht
in the *Morninside* chippie
I was confrontit by nae fewer than ten
o the reuchest and the teuchest
o yer haurdest-haurd haurd men
                – *and (O Gode!) hou I wished I was in Glasgow!*

Donald Campbell

IN FISHERROW

A hard north-easter fifty winters long
Has bronzed and shrivelled sere her face and neck;
Her locks are wild and grey, her teeth a wreck;
Her foot is vast, her bowed leg spare and strong.
A wide blue cloak, a squat and sturdy throng
Of curt blue coats, a mutch without a speck,
A white vest broidered black, her person deck,
Nor seems their picked, stern, old-world quaintness wrong.
Her great creel forehead-slung, she wanders nigh,
Easing the heavy strap with gnarled, brown fingers,
The spirit of traffic watchful in her eye,
Ever and anon imploring you to buy,
As looking down the street she onward lingers,
Reproachful, with a strange and doleful cry.

W. E. Henley

THE SONG OF HENRY COCKBURN

What could be more delightful
within a town? The sea of Bellevue foliage
gilded by the evening sun: the tumult
of blackbird and thrush sending
their morning notes into the blue
of summer air – this was his Edinburgh.
This way he would have it.

"On still nights I have stood, looked
at the prospect from Queen Street
gardens, and listened to
the corncraik's ceaseless rural call.
All Leith Walk was fully set with wood.
No Scotch city so graced with trees.
How can I forget the glory of the scene."
This is the way he would have it.

But that for money's sake blank
city walls broke off his views.
His war of words struck home.
Still Edinburgh was Edinburgh,
but that his continuum of protest
must end. Lord Cockburn now,
Senator of the College of Justice,
Judge. In silence he must sit
Through every city hurt.

But that his human heart prevailed
would do so until his end.
Ayr – his last circuit journey.
After the trial he noted: "One of the
finest days of this unsurpassed
Spring. The advancing sea insinuating
its clear waters irresistibly, yet gently.
There was no sound – a picture of repose."
Home – serenity in his ending.

No longer here to mark out right from wrong,
The Cockburn bears the burden of his song.

George Bruce

The Cockburn Association works to promote the conservation of Edinburgh's historic
and architectural heritage.

EDINBURGH: A PLACE OF MY OWN

If I had sat outside the Caledonian Hotel
this afternoon, cross-legged on the pavement,
with the restaurant wall behind me –

If I had placed a plastic cup in front of me
and a blanket round
my shoulders –

If the hours had been the east wind cutting
the length of Lothian Road, while
the cold hardened into me –

If the day could not have been different, or the date
or the clouds or the sleet
or the rain –

If I'd stopped looking round me at faces,
at people; if I'd stopped staring down
at my uncovered hands –

If I had been sitting up straight
when they asked me to move –

If I'd still been sitting up straight when they touched
my shoulders to wake me –

*

A woman. A plastic cup. A blanket.
The pavement.
The wall.

They told her she had to move on.
She said nothing.
They asked her her name.
She said nothing.

*

If a sheet had been used to cover my face –
If the post-code for where I'd been begging
were tagged to my foot –

That post-code would stand for my name
when, at last, I'd be given a place of my own.

Ron Butlin

Weather

What sound shall come but the old cry of the wind
In our inclement city?

Robert Louis Stevenson
from TO MY OLD FAMILIARS

from DOUBLE LIFE

This wind from Fife has cruel fingers, scooping
The heat from streets with salty finger-tips
Crusted with frost; and all Midlothian,
Stubborn against what heeled the sides of ships
Off from the Isle of May, stiffens its drooping
Branches to the south. Each man
And woman put their winter masks on, set
In a stony flinch, and only children can
Light with a scream an autumn fire that says
With the quick crackle of its smoky blaze,
"Summer's to burn and it's October yet".

My Water of Leith runs through a double city;
My city is threaded by a complex stream.
A matter for regret. If these cold stones
Could be stones only, and this watery gleam
Within the chasms of tenements and the pretty
Boskage of Dean could echo the groans
Of cart-wheeled bridges with only water's voice,
October would be just October. The bones
Of rattling winter would still lie underground,
Summer be less than ghost, I be unbound
From all the choking folderols of choice.

Norman MacCaig

WHAUR MAY THE WIN' DWALL?

Whaur may the win' dwall
That gars the lums o' Reekie rattle?
Comes it in frae Portingall,
Or owre the braid Atlantic?
A reel's in't, the Deil's in't,
A jig o' auld Satanas oh!
But when it ca's the lums doon
It's by wi' the romantic!

I ken its skelp upon my cheek,
Its jockteleg upon my thrapple,
It fills wi' blasphemy the meek,
Wi' girns the Adam's apple;
A dag on't, a drag on't,
The fairies built Dunedin oh,
The Deil he tries to blaw it doon,
And wow! But he's succeedin' oh!

Lewis Spence

gars	makes
lums	chimneys
ca's	brings
skelp	slap
jockteleg	pocket knife
thrapple	throat
dag on't	confound it
Dunedin	Edinburgh

NOVEMBER NIGHT, EDINBURGH

The night tinkles like ice in glasses.
Leaves are glued to the pavement with frost.
The brown air fumes at the shop windows,
Tries the doors, and sidles past.

I gulp down winter raw. The heady
Darkness swirls with tenements.
In a brown fuzz of cottonwool
Lamps fade up crags, die into pits.

Frost in my lungs is harsh as leaves
Scraped up on paths. – I look up, there,
A high roof sails, at the mast-head
Fluttering a grey and ragged star.

The world's a bear shrugged in his den.
It's snug and close in the snoring night.
And outside like chrysanthemums
The fog unfolds its bitter scent.

Norman MacCaig

HAIKU

Edinburgh
in winter; the McEwan Hall
dreams of Italy

Angela McSeveney

from TO THE PHIZ. AN ODE

Look up to Pentland's towring taps,
Buried beneath great wreaths of snaw,
O'er ilka cleugh, ilk scar and slap,
As high as ony Roman wa'.

Driving their baws frae whins or tee,
There's no ae gowfer to be seen,
Nor dousser fowk wysing a jee
The byas bouls on Tamson's green.

Then fling on coals, and ripe the ribs,
And beek the house baith butt and ben,
That mutchkin stoup it hads but dribs,
Then let's get in the tappit hen.

Good claret best keeps out the cauld,
And drives away the winter soon,
It makes a man baith gash and bauld,
And heaves his saul beyond the moon.

Allan Ramsay

cleugh	*ravine*
dousser	*more sedate*
wysing a jee	*leaning to one side*
byas bouls	*bowls*
ripe the ribs	*poke the grate*
beek	*warm up*
baith butt and ben	*from end to end*
mutchkin stoup	*English pint pot*
dribs	*drops*
tappit hen	*Scots quart jug*
gash	*wise*

EDINBURGH UNDER SNOW

First Day

We're with the drunkards
taking a white walk at three a.m.
falling in a room filled with feathers.

Snow! It runs into all our corners
and sets like aspic
and covers every hope and desire.

We breathe, mixed with ice, an air
blue as polar bears' tongues.
Tenements tip our iceberg.

Where is the true town? With
whiteout, no whereabouts, the only
brightness comes from the ground.

An old man is strolling
along the centre of the road, playing
his mouth-organ in Tollcross.

The earth first cools by night:
we learn to be ductile, yielding,
under the influence of white.

Last Day

Babylon's rebuilt in virgin stone.
We see her underpinnings
through torn paper snow.

Pavements are a stiff new sight;
through tufted wastes of old ice
grow specious streets and shops again.

She's back after a fortnight,
our city, under a sky with cloud,
her face skimmed of makeup.

She's got a spark
from our tinderbox world,
a going smoke.

Once more the staggered figures
struggling, falling, digging out,
reach the day's targets.

Now we're the same:
obdurate, impenetrable,
night's black again.

Valerie Gillies

EDINBURGH COURTYARD IN JULY

Hot light is smeared as thick as paint
On these ramshackle tenements. Stones smell
    Of dust. Their hoisting into quaint
Crowsteps, corbels, carved with fool and saint,
Holds fathoms of heat, like water in a well.

Cliff-dwellers have poked out from their
High cave-mouths brilliant rags on drying-lines;
    They hang still, dazzling in the glare,
And lead the eye up, ledge by ledge, to where
A chimney's tilted helmet winks and shines.

And water from a broken drain
Splashes a glassy hand out in the air
    That breaks in an unbraiding rain
And falls still fraying, to become a stain
That spreads by footsteps, ghosting everywhere.

Norman MacCaig

Double City

City of everywhere, broken necklace in the sun,
You are caves of guilt, you are pinnacles of jubilation.

Norman MacCaig
from DROP-OUT IN EDINBURGH

from POEMS 1869–1876: VII

I walk the streets smoking my pipe
And I love the dallying shop-girl
That leans with rounded stern to look at the fashions;
And I hate the bustling citizen,
The eager and hurrying man of affairs I hate,
Because he bears his intolerance writ on his face
And every movement and word of him tells me how much he
hates me.

I love night in the city,
The lighted streets and the swinging gait of harlots.
I love cool pale morning,
In the empty bye-streets,
With only here and there a female figure,
A slavey with lifted dress and the key in her hand,
A girl or two at play in a corner of a waste-land
Tumbling and showing their legs and crying out to me loosely.

Robert Louis Stevenson

from EMBRO TO THE PLOY

In simmer, whan aa sorts foregether
in Embro, to the ploy,
fowk seek out friens to hae a blether,
or faes they'd fain annoy;
smorit wi British Railways' reek
frae Glesca or Glen Roy
or Wick, they come to hae a week
of cultivatit joy,
                    or three,
in Embro to the ploy …

The auld High Schule, whaur monie a skelp
of triple-tonguit tawse
has gien a hyst-up and a help
towards Doctorates of Laws,
nou hears, for Ramsay's cantie rhyme,
loud pawmies of applause
frae folk that pey a pund a time
to sit on wudden raws
                    gey hard
in Embro to the ploy.

The haly kirk's Assembly-haa
nou fairly coups the creel
wi Lindsay's *Three Estaitis*, braw
devices of the Deil.
About our heids the satire stots
like hailstanes till we reel;
the bawrs are in auld-farrant Scots,
it's maybe jist as weill,
                    imphm,
in Embro to the ploy.

Robert Garioch

Embro	*Edinburgh*
ploy	*frolic, fun*
blether	*chat*
faes	*foes*
smorit	*smothered*
reek	*smoke*
tawse	*belt*
pawmies	*claps*
coups	*upsets*
stots	*bounces*
bawrs	*jokes*
auld-farrant	*old-fashioned*

BUDDHA

I met the Buddha in Edinburgh:
hunkered in a doorway in the West Bow,
a can of Carlsberg in his hand.

Around him shops, cops and dogs
were doing their miserable business.
He was doing his:

with a hand as black as a tenement
he wiped his oracular mouth,
growled his simple teachings:

Fuck-all point. Fuck-all point.
Lost the lot. Lost the lot.
Guid riddance. Guid riddance.

And he watched me, the nothing I was
as I passed. He watches me still
crouched in a doorway in my mind

in that inelegant, Scottish half-lotus,
the void of the afternoon
in the void of his eyes.

Brian McCabe

CHORAL SYMPHONY

The customary conversation
Gives way to applause
For the Orchestra. Then
A roar, as Karajan
Takes the stand. He raises
His baton; the strings sweep in.

During the interval, we remain
Seated. Two Edinburgh ladies
Behind us complain:
"Such Teutonic discipline
Breeds perfection,
Not Art." Their companion agrees.

At the end they join in,
As the ovation goes on
And on. What has changed their tune?
We overhear: "Weren't the Chorus
Superb!" "As one voice."
"And that lace, on Muriel's dress."

Stewart Conn

FESTIVAL CITY: YON TIME AGAIN

Consider this young, defiantly *un*-Oxbridge playwright
Dreaming of how Stoppard's life was quite transformed by
  Rosencrantz
Last night, OK they had an audience of eight, but really they
  might
Be grateful not to have to toady to mere sycophants!
Theatre, for him, is Language – the what-to-say, the way-to-say
  right
(At the very name of "Mime" his kekks just squirm with ants)
But what did the *Scotsman* mean: "attempts both lyrical and
  splenetic"?
Was it entirely a compliment to say "alternately Brechtian and
  frenetic"?

Mauled by savage critics, the student company pleads mitigating
  factors
(Philistine audiences, the lighting-lady's *minor* faff).
Naff stand-up comics, despite feminist detractors,
Still malign the missus, would slag their grannies for a laugh.
Knackered Veteran Fringe Director/Actors
Long for just a half-hour's kip before the Half.
Wine bars' tills are ringing, and our ears with Theatre Talk
("Jeremy! Jesus, I haven't seen you since Le Coq!")

While Real Year-Round Young Edinburghers sip Camparis
Quaintly – yet familiarly – in some tent.
Demand of each other (in the kind of tone that carries)
Now it's Yon Time again, where last year went?
Once again they meant this year to let the flat and bugger off to
  Paris,
Barcelona (or better) on the proceeds of This Three Weeks'
  Rent –
Except: some horror-commune-theatre-company's drunken
  pukes and shittings
Might prove really ruinous to furniture and fittings.

So, mibbe, in the long run, Being Here is for the best.
They *definitely* are going to go to *something* – once they know
    what's Kosher
And what's Quoted. This year again they tote the diary for
    Bookfest,
Five Official Festival Programmes, the fatter-than-ever Fringe
    Brochure
Plus a confusion of hot-neon handbills and hyping flyers pressed,
Like religious tracts, on them by devotees. Yet they're not so sure
– Despite flourishing Fringe Sundays and sunnyday floats at
    Opening Parades
Whether the Fringe'll ever be the same post Assembly Rooms,
    post Aids.

Liz Lochhead

FIN DE FESTIVAL: EDINBURGH 2000

Edinburgh rediscovers its classic grey –
most delicious of lourdness, an ecstasy of glum.
The trendy standups from London have been and come
and gone, and their posters remain to be torn down.
Yet echoes of Czech brass linger in the town,
wisps of luxurious violin,
and phantoms of airborne dancers tempt to sin
the time-preened matriarch who resumes her sway.

Angus Calder

NEMO CANEM IMPUNE LACESSIT

I kicked an Edinbro dug-luver's dug,
leastweys I tried; my timing wes owre late.
It stopped whit it wes daein til my gate
and skelpit aff to find some ither mug.

Whit a sensation! If a clockwark thug
suid croun ye wi a brolly owre yir pate,
the Embro folk wad leave ye til yir fate;
it's you, maist like, wad get a flee in yir lug.

But kick the Friend of Man! Or hae a try!
The Friend of Wummin, even, that's faur waur
a felony, mair dangerous forbye.

Meddle wi puir dumb craiturs gin ye daur;
that maks ye a richt cruel bruit, my! my!
And whit d'ye think yir braw front yett is for?

Robert Garioch

skelpit	*scampered*
faur waur	*far worse*
gin ye daur	*if you dare*
yett	*gate*

from FLORET SILVA UNDIQUE

Floret silva undique
The lily, the rose, the rose I lay.

Tell-tale leaves on the elm-tree bole;
Reekie's oot for a Sabbath stroll.
Tim and Eck from their pad in Sciennes –
Cowboy T-shirts and Brutus jeans;
Gobstopper Gib and Jakie Tar,
Billies oot the Victoria Bar,
And Davie Bowie plyin' his trade
The sweetest minstrel was ever laid.
Floret silva undique
The rocker, the ring and the gowans gay.
The bonniest pair ye iver seen
Play chasie on the Meedies green.
Undressed to the nines, frae tit tae toe,
The Kimmers o' Coogate are a' on show.
Ripper o' flies, lord o' the tools,
Yon mental boot boy Eros rules.

Floret silva undique
We'll hae a ball, though the Deil's to pay.
The quick and the slaw are game for a tear;
Sma'back snooves from his Greyfriars lair.
Out of the darkmans the queer coves come,
Janus guisers from bield and tomb:
Scrunchit hurdies and raw-bone heid
Junkies mell wi' the livin deid.
Get stuck in, Hornie, and show's the way.
The lily, the rose, the rose I lay.

Hamish Henderson

billies	*pals*
gowans	*daisies*
Meedies	*The Meadows (park)*
kimmers	*lassies*
Sma'back	*Death*
darkmans	*night*
guisers	*masqueraders*
bield	*shelter*
hurdies	*thighs*

EDINBURGH

Bound in lambswool, tweed and foxfur,
skin as pale as her antimacassar,
my landlady sits on the edge of her seat
to announce a rise in the rent.

The east wind tousles her drying-green,
but everything indoors is in place.
The wallpaper is a regiment of roses,
marching round a newly-crowned Queen.

She picks a scone from a tartan tin,
and nibbles. "*Everything is going up.
It's regrettable ...*" And her lips impart
a lobster kiss to the bone-china cup.

She learned this poise with a book on her head,
but it's capital that keeps it high.
Her bank's no castle in the air,
but a church grounded in rock.

The keys of my house are in her purse,
and the law's on her side of the case.
Cushioned on her couch, without an ashtray,
all I can see is my lengthening ash.

Gerald Mangan

Dear Edinburgh

Dear city of my heart, to whom
I'm vowed in all your moods and tenses ...

Peter Taylor
from TO EDINBURGH

JEAN BRODIE'S CHILDREN

Jean Brodie's children in your small green caps,
I hear you twitter down the avenues.

The great round bells ring out, the Mademoiselle
despairs of English. In the rustling dorms
you giggle under sheets.

"Dear Edinburgh, how I remember you,
your winter cakes and tea, your bright red fire,
your swirling cloaks and clouds.

Your grammar and your Greek, the hush of leaves,
No Orchids for Miss Blandish with a torch
beneath the tweedy blanket.

Ah, those beautiful days, all green and shady,
our black and pleated skirts, our woollen stockings,
our ties of a calm mauve.

Mistresses, iron in their certainty,
their language unambiguous but their lives
trembling on grey boughs."

Iain Crichton Smith

from KYND KITTOCK'S LAND

– I'll tell ye what I say, and what I ken.
This auld rortie city that ye speak o',
(Ken) here we'll be and here we'll bide
Come wind, high water and the westren gales –
I've been here, and will be, year on year,
Five hunder year or thereabouts
And I'll be here five hunder yet to come, at the world's end.
Embro toun is me and me is it – d'ye see?
The winds will come as winds have been
But ever and aye there's us
That sits here bien and snog,
Members, son, o' an auld companie
In an auld rortie city –
Wretched, tae, ye cried us, ach, young man,
Ye ken nocht aboot it – as ye said yersel.

Times aye cheynge and this auld runt
Will flouer again (Heh! Heh! Yon's me!)
And hae nae cheynge ava – we're aye the same,
The desperate and the deid, the livin raucle yins,
D'ye ken? Ay, though, and sae it is,
Auld Reekie through the keekin glass
Looks fine, and sae it does.
        And the mornin and the evenin
        Were anither age gane by …

I'm getting gey an' auld, and wearie …
Sleepie … my grey heid hings …

And shall she get the richts o' it,
A diadem for the brou?
Shall Scotland croun her ain again,
This ancient capital – ?
Or sell the thing for scrap?
Or some Yankee museum maybe?
I'll be here bidin the answer …
Here I be and here I drink,
This is mine, Kynd Kittock's land,
For ever and aye while stane shall stand –
For ever and aye till the World's End.

Sydney Goodsir Smith

ken	*you know*
bien	*comfortable*
raucle	*robust*

Kynd Kittock is the subject of a ballad attributed to William Dunbar ... she now looks
after the alehouse situated just outside the gates of Paradise. (S.G.S)

from AULD REIKIE

    Reikie, fareweel! I ne'er could part
Wi thee but wi a dowy heart.
Aft frae the Fifan coast I've seen
Thee tow'ring on thy summit green;
So glowr the saints when first is given
A fav'rite keek o' glore and heaven:
On earth nae mair they bend their een,
But quick assume angelic mien;
So I on Fife wad glowr no more,
But gallop'd to Edina's shore.

Robert Fergusson

dowy	*sad*
glowr	*gaze*
keek	*peep*

ENVOI

Gin I were ta'en awa
To fremit pairts unkent,
Though nae cauld winds should blaw
I wadna be content.

The Auld Toun's silhouette
Etched on a lift o' leid –
Gin *yon* I could forget
I shairly wad be deid.

Deid? But my ghaist micht sune
Return like moth to flame
And jink aboot the toun
Weel satisfied – at hame!

Douglas Fraser

fremit	*foreign*
lift o' leid	*leaden sky*
gin	*if*
jink	*frolic*

FAREWEEL, EDINBURGH

Fareweel, Edinburgh, where happy we hae been,
Fareweel, Edinburgh, Caledonia's Queen!
Auld Reekie, fare-ye-weel, and Reekie New beside,
Ye're like a chieftain grim and grey, wi' a young bonny bride.
Fareweel, Edinburgh, and your trusty volunteers,
Your Council a' sae circumspect, your Provost without peers,
Your stately College stuff'd wi' lear, your rantin' High-Schule yard;
The jib, the lick, the roguish trick, the ghaists o' auld toun-guard.

Fareweel, Edinburgh, your philosophic men;
Your scribes that set you a' tae richts, and wield the golden pen;
The Session-court, your thrang resort, bigwigs and lang gowns a';
And if ye dinna keep the peace, it's no for want of law.
Fareweel, Edinburgh, and a' your glittering wealth;
Your Bernard's Well, your Calton Hill, where every breeze is health;
An' spite o' a' your fresh sea-gales, should ony chance to dee,
It's no for want o' recipe, the doctor, or the fee.

Fareweel, Edinburgh, your hospitals and ha's,
The rich man's friend, the Cross lang ken'd, auld Ports, and city wa's;
The Kirks that grace their honoured place, now peacefu' as they stand,
Where'er they're found, on Scottish ground, the bulwarks of the land.
Fareweel, Edinburgh, your sons o' genius fine,
That send your name on wings o' fame beyond the burnin' line;
A name that's stood maist since the flood, and just when it's forgot,
Your bard will be forgotten too, your ain Sir Walter Scott.

Fareweel Edinburgh, and a' your daughters fair;
Your Palace in the sheltered glen, your Castle in the air;
Your rocky brows, your grassy knowes, and eke your mountain bauld;
Were I to tell your beauties a', my tale would ne'er be tauld.
Now, fareweel, Edinburgh, where happy we hae been;
Fareweel, Edinburgh, Caledonia's Queen!
Prosperity to Edinburgh wi' every risin' sun,
And blessin's be on Edinburgh, till time his race has run!

Carolina, Lady Nairne

lear	*learning, education*
rantin'	*roistering*
thrang	*crowded*
eke	*also*

AULD REEKIE

When chitterin' cauld the day sall daw,
Loud may your bonny bugles blaw
    And loud your drums may beat.
Hie owre the land at evenfa'
Your lamps may glitter raw by raw,
    Along the gowsty street.

I gang nae mair whaur ance I gaed,
By Brunston, Fairmileheid, or Braid;
    But far frae Kirk and Tron.
O still, ayont the muckle sea,
Still are ye dear, and dear to me,
    Auld Reekie, still and on!

Robert Louis Stevenson

| chitterin' | shivering |
| ayont | beyond |

BIOGRAPHICAL NOTES

MARGOT ROBERT ADAMSON (1898–?) translated early Scots and English poetry from the Bannatyne and other manuscripts into modern English in *A Treasury of Middle-English Verse* (Dent, 1930). In her own poetry she touches on Edinburgh and East Lothian, notably in *A Northern Holiday* (1928). She also wrote novels, and travel literature "for those who stay at home".

JAMES BALLANTINE (1808–1877) Despite a disadvantaged childhood in the West Port, and some years spent as a house painter, James Ballantine became an exponent of the revival of glass painting, and was commissioned to execute the stained-glass windows in the House of Lords; his windows are still to be seen in the kirks of Greyfriars and St Giles. A great admirer of Robert Burns, he himself wrote unpretentious popular verses in local dialect, and published several books of his own poetry between the 1840s and the 1870s. Ballantine was energetic in his support of the building of the Scott Monument and other projects in the city.

MEG BATEMAN (b.1959) Born near Edinburgh, Meg Bateman's family moved into the New Town, and she was brought up and educated in the city. A degree in Gaelic at Aberdeen University was followed by a PhD in medieval Gaelic religious poetry, and teaching Celtic Studies at Aberdeen. She now lives on Skye and teaches at Sabhal Mòr Ostaig. *Aotromachd agus Dàin Eile / Lightness and Other Poems* (1997), won a Scottish Arts Council award, and *Soirbheas / Fair Wind* was published by Polygon in 2007.

NORMAN BISSETT (b.1938) studied literature at Aberdeen and Yale Universities, and linguistics at Lancaster. He worked for the British Council for thirty years, in various parts of the world. Since retiring in 1995, he has produced several small poetry books, the most recent being *Langass* (Poetry Monthly Press, 2006). He now lives in Edinburgh, and has been president of the Edinburgh Writers' Club.

ALEXANDER BOSWELL (1775–1822) Alexander Boswell became Laird of Auchinleck at the age of twenty, upon the death of his father, James. A model landowner, he was also an amateur printer, a literary antiquary, a poet and songwriter. Having married an Edinburgh lady, Boswell was no stranger to the place, and wrote several poems which look back to the city as it was a half-century before. His efforts in maintaining civil order in Ayrshire during the troubled decade preceding the Reform Act were rewarded with a baronetcy in 1821, but he was killed the following year in one of the last duels to take place in Britain, over the authorship of a political satire.

133

GEORGE BRUCE (1909–2002) was born and brought up in Fraserburgh; the landscape and sea of the north-east of Scotland are mirrored in his sparse, telling poems. He was a producer with BBC radio for thirty years, in Aberdeen and Edinburgh. *Today Tomorrow: The Collected Poems of George Bruce 1933–2000* was published by Polygon in 2001, but he kept writing up until his death; *Through the Letterbox*, a collaboration with artist Elizabeth Blackadder, appeared posthumously in 2003, as did a small collection of his local poems, put together by his neighbours in Warriston Crescent. He was awarded the OBE in 1984.

RON BUTLIN (b.1949) Born in Edinburgh and educated at Dumfries Academy and the University of Edinburgh, Ron Butlin now lives again in Edinburgh and writes full-time: poetry, fiction, journalism, and opera libretti. He was Scottish / Canadian Exchange Fellow at the University of New Brunswick in the 1980s, and has held residencies at the Universities of Edinburgh, Stirling and St Andrews, at schools in Edinburgh, and at the National Gallery of Scotland. His collections include *Histories of Desire* (Bloodaxe, 1995) and *Without a Backward Glance* (Barzan, 2005).

ANGUS CALDER (b.1942) Historian, journalist, editor and critic, Angus Calder has held academic posts in Britain and as far afield as New Zealand and Zimbabwe, and has lived in Edinburgh for the past twenty years. A prolific author of works on socio-political themes, he has also always written poetry, bringing out his first book, *Waking in Waikato* (diehard) in 1997. His latest book, *Sun Behind the Castle: Edinburgh Poems* (Luath, 2004), includes versions from the works of Roman poet Horace, updated to present-day Edinburgh, and set in Tollcross.

DONALD CAMPBELL (b.1940) Born in Caithness, Donald Campbell is a poet, playwright, stage director and theatre historian who has lived in Edinburgh all his working life. His own drama has won three *Scotsman* Fringe First awards for productions at the Edinburgh Festival Fringe, and much of it – notably *Blackfriars Wynd* (1980) – brings old Edinburgh to life. Many of his poems are centred on Edinburgh and his life in it (*Selected Poems: 1970–1990*, Galliard). He has most recently written the guide to Edinburgh in the *Cities of the Imagination* series (Signal Books, 2003). He was the William Soutar Fellow in Perth, 1991–1993, and Royal Literary Fund Fellow at Napier University, 2000–2002.

"CLAUDERO" (JAMES WILSON, *c.*1730–1789) A native of Cumbernauld, James Wilson lived in Edinburgh for over thirty years. A satirist by profession, he made part of his living by producing squibs on the great and good of the day. His talents were put to better use in several poems which appeared in *Miscellanies in Prose and Verse* (1766) in which he used the

134

sharp side of his pen to remonstrate against the demolition of various edifices – the Netherbow and the Royal Porch of Holyrood House, as well as the Cross.

STEWART CONN (b.1936) Though a west-of-Scotland man by birth, Stewart Conn has lived in Edinburgh for many years. He was head of radio drama for BBC Scotland from 1977–1992, and is the author of nine collections of poetry, the most recent being *Ghosts at Cockcrow* (Bloodaxe, 2005). He was appointed the first Edinburgh City Makar in 2002; while in office his works included "poem-posters" for Edinburgh buses and editing a collection commissioned for the Royal College of Surgeons quincentenary celebrations. He helped make the case, in verse, for Edinburgh's successful bid to become the first UNESCO City of Literature. In 2006 he edited *100 Favourite Scottish Poems* (Luath), and also in that year was awarded the inaugural Iain Crichton Smith Award for services to literature.

CHRISTINE DE LUCA (b.1947) was born and brought up in Shetland, and has lived in Edinburgh for forty years. She writes in both Shetlandic and English, and has done much work in translating poets of various nationalities into her native tongue. Her own poems have been translated into several languages, and published in both national and international magazines. Her fourth collection, *Parallel Worlds*, was published by Luath in 2005; she is currently working on story-books and CDs for children in Shetlandic. She has collaborated across the arts, and been an active member of Shore Poets in Edinburgh for many years.

WILLIAM DUNBAR (c.1460–c.1513) may be considered Edinburgh's first poet – certainly the first to depict so vividly, and so truthfully, the state of the city. He was born in the Lothians, attended the University of St Andrews, and took priest's orders, but held a position in the court of James IV in the later decades of his life. His poetic virtuosity ranged from vituperative "flyting", comedy and satire, to a petition in verse for an increase in salary from the king, and the poignant "Lament for the Makaris".

ROBERT FERGUSSON (1750–1774) was born in Edinburgh, and apart from time at school in Dundee and at university in St Andrews, spent his short life in the city – a life spent observing and writing. Although at the time most educated Scots used English, it was in an assured and vibrant Scots that Fergusson chose to depict the Edinburgh of the 1770s in all its noise and colour and smell. He is credited with re-establishing Scots as a literary language, and was a major influence on Robert Burns. His masterpiece, the long poem "Auld Reikie", was left unfinished by his sad decline into depression and ill-health, followed by his early death in the Bedlam at the age of twenty-four.

DOUGLAS FRASER (1910–1996) Although his contribution to the promotion of poetry in Edinburgh was considerable – he served on the committee of Scottish PEN, and worked for the Edinburgh Poetry Club and Poetry Association of Scotland – Douglas Fraser will always be fondly remembered for the good-humoured poems through which he takes an affectionate look at the foibles of his beloved native city. *Rhymes o' Auld Reekie* (Macdonald, 1973) was the second of four books of poetry published fairly late in life; Fraser worked most of his life in an assurance company, and his poems began to appear in magazines in the late fifties. He was awarded the Queen's Silver Jubilee Medal in 1977.

ROBERT GARIOCH (1909–1981) Like Robert Fergusson, a poet with whom he acknowledged great empathy, Garioch wrote of the street life of Edinburgh in a lively Scots which was well matched to his sharp observations on the manners of the city's inhabitants. He was also master of the art of translation into Scots, notably in his versions of the sonnets of Giuseppe Belli. Garioch returned to Edinburgh after retiring from teaching in England, worked at the School of Scottish Studies, and was Writing Fellow at the University of Edinburgh from 1971 to 1973. A new edition of his *Collected Poems* was brought out by Polygon in 2004.

VALERIE GILLIES (b.1948) became the second Edinburgh City Makar in 2005. A freelance writer since 1971, with eight collections of poetry, she gained a Creative Scotland award for *The Spring Teller*, a book of poems inspired by Scotland's springs, a project that included exploring Edinburgh's springs and wells. Well known as "the river poet", who followed the Tweed and the Tay from source to the sea, Valerie Gillies has edited the Scottish Poetry Library's poetry map of Scotland, and has done much collaborative work with artists, notably poem-inscriptions with different sculptors in sites across southern Scotland.

GEORGE CAMPBELL HAY / DEORSA MAC IAIN DHEORSA (1915–1984) It was his childhood in Argyllshire that gave Hay his linguistic background: he wrote in Gaelic, Scots and English, and translated much European poetry into Gaelic. He was sent to board at Fettes College in Edinburgh when ten, and lived again in the city for many years in later life. Hay was a staunch Scottish nationalist and a conscientious objector, although he eventually served in North Africa and Italy, which contributed to his physical and mental ill health. He was a recognised figure of the Scottish literary renaissance; his work certainly was most significant in the renaissance of Gaelic poetry in the twentieth century. His *Collected Poems and Songs* was published by Edinburgh University Press in 2000.

HAMISH HENDERSON (1919–2002) Poet, songwriter and folklorist Hamish Henderson was born in Blairgowrie, Perthshire. He worked for the School of Scottish Studies at the University of Edinburgh from the 1950s as a field researcher and collector of traditional songs, and was himself a leading figure of the Scottish folk revival, notably with the Edinburgh People's Festivals in the early 1950s. His experience of war in North Africa led to the publication of *Elegies for the Dead in Cyrenaica* (John Lehmann, 1948); his *Collected Poems and Songs* were published by Curly Snake in 2000.

W. E. HENLEY (1849–1903) Editor, essayist and critic, W. E. Henley came to Edinburgh to be treated by Professor Lister for tubercular arthritis. His two-year stay in the old Royal Infirmary led to the two things for which he is mostly remembered today: the writing of his poem "Invictus", and his friendship with Robert Louis Stevenson, who famously took Henley as his model for Long John Silver. A strong character and rather fierce critic, Henley was also fierce in his support of many emerging literary figures of the time, and published Kipling and Conrad among others.

ALEXANDER HUTCHISON (b.1943) was born in Buckie, worked for eighteen years in the USA and Canada, and now lives in Glasgow. A university lecturer by profession, he is also a poet and translator in Scots and English. A poem of his was engraved on stone in the birthplace of Cicero as part of the international project *Il Libro di Pietro*; his most recent publication is *Carbon Atom* (Link-light, 2006).

LIZ LOCHHEAD (b.1947) has firmly established her reputation as one of the country's leading poets and as a popular performer of her own poetry. She studied and taught art in Glasgow before becoming a full-time writer, publishing her first collection of poems, *Memo for Spring*, in 1972. Also a playwright, her adaptation of Euripides' *Medea* (2000) won the Saltire Society's Scottish Book of the Year Award. *The Colour of Black & White: Poems 1984–2003* was published by Polygon in 2003. She became Glasgow's Poet Laureate in 2005.

NORMAN MACCAIG (1910–1996) was born in Edinburgh, where he worked for many years as a primary-school teacher. From *Riding Lights* in 1955 to *Voice Over* in 1988, he published fourteen collections of poetry. He was appointed a fellow in Creative Writing at Edinburgh in 1967, and in 1970 he became a reader in poetry at the University of Stirling. For most of his life, MacCaig divided his time between Edinburgh and Assynt in the north-west Highlands; the landscape of Assynt and the townscapes of Edinburgh are recurring themes of his poetry. *The Poems of Norman MacCaig* was published by Polygon in 2005. He was awarded the Queen's Medal for Poetry in 1986.

HUGH MACDIARMID (1892–1978) is generally acknowledged to be Scotland's most influential and controversial writer of the twentieth century. He was born in Dumfriesshire, and after war service worked as a journalist in various parts of Scotland, settling near Biggar for his last years. He was a founding member of the National Party of Scotland, and was a supporter of Communism; his masterpiece *A Drunk Man Looks at the Thistle* (1926) combines his nationalism and internationalism. MacDiarmid was a multi-faceted character whose poetry, journalism and criticism cannot be overestimated in terms of the effect they had on sparking the Scottish literary renaissance into life.

STUART MACGREGOR (1935–1973) A novelist, poet and physician who studied medicine at the University of Edinburgh, Stuart MacGregor died in an accident while working at the university in Kingston, Jamaica. His poetry was first collected in the anthology *Four Points of a Saltire* (1970), and *Poems and Songs* was published posthumously by Macdonald in 1974. With Hamish Henderson, he established the University of Edinburgh Folk Song Society, and his own songs remain popular.

DUNCAN BÀN MACINTYRE / DONNCHADH BAN MAC AN T-SAOIR (1724–1812) The first half of Duncan Bàn's life was spent in or near his native Argyllshire, where his poetry soared to great heights with pieces like "Moladh Bheinn Dhoran / In Praise of Ben Doran" – poems of superb description of the glens and hills where he was a gamekeeper. He moved to Edinburgh in 1767, and became a constable in the City Guard. He is buried in Greyfriars Kirkyard, and there is a monument to him overlooking Loch Awe.

BRIAN MCCABE (b.1951) Born in a mining community near Edinburgh, Brian McCabe studied Philosophy and English Literature at the University of Edinburgh, which is where he started writing poetry; *One Atom to Another* appeared in 1987, and *Body Parts* in 1999. He is also a novelist and short-story writer, his books having won several Scottish Arts Council book awards. He has been the William Soutar Fellow, is now writer in residence at the University of Edinburgh, and edits the *Edinburgh Review*.

ANGELA MCSEVENEY (b.1964) was brought up in the Borders and elsewhere, moved to the city in 1982 to attend the University of Edinburgh, and still lives in the city. She has worked in libraries, as a museum assistant on the Royal Mile, and is now a personal care assistant. She is a member of Edinburgh's Shore Poets. Her publications are *Coming Out With It* (Polygon, 1992), and *Imprint* (*Edinburgh Review*, 2002).

GERALD MANGAN (b.1951) Glasgow-born Mangan has lived and worked in various parts of Scotland and Ireland, and in France, where he now resides. He is a poet, cartoonist, playwright and journalist, having been resident playwright at Theatre Workshop in Edinburgh in the mid 1970s, and later poet in residence at Dundee's College of Art; he now writes and illustrates for the *Times Literary Supplement* and other journals. His collection *Waiting for the Storm* was published by Bloodaxe in 1990.

LADY NAIRNE (Carolina Oliphant) (1766–1845) Scotland's greatest songstress, Lady Nairne was the author of many beautiful songs often today thought of as traditional. The daughter of a staunchly Jacobite family, she wrote in sympathy to the cause, setting her songs to old tunes. Marriage to Major William Murray Nairne brought her to Edinburgh, where she carried on her "queer trade of song-writing" under a pseudonym, keeping it secret even from her husband. *Lays from Strathearn* appeared under her own name, posthumously, in 1846.

WILL H. OGILVIE (1869–1963) is a poet who won great popularity both in his native Borders and in Australia, where he worked as a young man on sheep stations, and where he is given national status as a balladeer of the bush. He wrote copiously, his work ranging widely from hymns of praise to his beloved Borders, to sporting verse (he is the undoubted master poet of the horse) and witty lines contributed to *Punch*. Will Ogilvie's ashes were scattered on the road to Roberton – the site of one of his most famous poems – and a memorial was erected in 1993.

JOHN W. OLIVER (1893–1957) Apart from service during the First World War, John W. Oliver spent his life in Edinburgh, as a teacher of English at Daniel Stewart's College, and Principal Lecturer in English at Moray House Teacher Training College. He was joint editor of several books and anthologies, author of many school texts, and produced one pamphlet of poems mostly concerned with (and poking gentle fun at) the life and characters of his native city. He was chairman of the Saltire Society, and president of several Burns' clubs.

ALLAN RAMSAY (1685–1758) Born in Lanarkshire, Ramsay moved to Edinburgh in 1700 to become an apprentice to a wigmaker, although he eventually gave up wigmaking for things more literary when he opened a bookshop and circulating library in the Luckenbooths. His first book of poems was published in 1721; his pastoral comedy *The Gentle Shepherd* was very well received, but it was his earthy poetry in Scots about Edinburgh's taverns and everyday life that earned him great and lasting popularity in the city.

TESSA RANSFORD (b.1938) worked for two decades to set up and sustain the School of Poets and the Scottish Poetry Library (before retiring at the millennium), for which services she was awarded an OBE. She also spent a decade editing *Lines Review*. She continues as a freelance poetry adviser and practitioner, works to encourage the publication of poetry in pamphlet form and has been president of Scottish PEN. The most recent of her eleven books of poetry is *When it Works it Feels Like Play* (Ramsay Head, 1998), followed by a series of pamphlet selections from Akros. She has lived in Edinburgh for most of her life.

JAMES ROBERTSON (b.1958) is a poet, novelist, and editor. His poetry pamphlet *Stirling Sonnets* won the Callum Macdonald Memorial Award in 2002. He compiled a new edition of Robert Fergusson's selected poems in 2000, marking the 250th anniversary of the poet's birth, and is general editor of the Scots language imprint Itchy Coo. His novel *Joseph Knight* (Fourth Estate, 2003) won both the Saltire and the Scottish Arts Council Book of the Year awards. In November 2004 he was the first writer in residence at the Scottish Parliament, and consequently published *Voyage of Intent: Sonnets and Essays from the Scottish Parliament* (Luath, 2005).

ROBIN ROBERTSON (b.1955) was born in the north-east of Scotland. He has spent over twenty years working in publishing, currently at Jonathan Cape. His poetry collections are *A Painted Field* (Picador, 1997), which won several prizes, including the Saltire Society Scottish First Book of the Year award, and most recently *Swithering*, which won the 2006 Forward Prize. Although he now lives in London, the landscape of much of his poetry remains Scottish.

ALEXANDER SCOTT (1920–1989) was born and brought up in Aberdeen. He taught at the Universities of Edinburgh and Glasgow, working to establish the Department of Scottish Literature at the latter, and was equally committed to the development of the study of Scottish literature in schools. He edited several anthologies of poetry and wrote critical works on poets (most notably *Still Life*, the biography of William Soutar). He wrote in both English and in a powerful literary Scots enriched by some of the vocabulary of his native Aberdeenshire. His *Collected Poems* was published in 1994.

SIR WALTER SCOTT (1771–1832) The giant of Scottish literature was an Edinburgh man, born in the Old Town and brought up in George Square, and the city features in both his prose and poetry. Some years spent in the Borders as a child gave him a taste for the ballads and stories which furnished the background for his narrative poetry and historical novels. Scott's was a life led with great energy, his daily work as a lawyer hindering neither his enormous literary output, his enthusiasm for reviving old customs, nor his major achievement of gathering the Border ballads into the *Minstrelsy of the Scottish Borders*.

IAIN CRICHTON SMITH (1928–1998) was born on the island of Lewis, and spent most of his life as a schoolteacher in Glasgow and Oban, receiving an OBE in 1980. From *The Long River* (Macdonald, 1955) to *A Country for Old Men* (Carcanet, 2000), he was a prolific writer of poetry and fiction in both English and Gaelic; a sense of exile is at the heart of his work. His view of Scotland's culture, small communities and religion was never romantic, but he had a keen eye for small delights and a strong sense of wonder.

JAMES SMITH (1824–1887) A writer who was amazingly popular in his lifetime (his *Poems, Songs and Ballads* went through four editions), James Smith was so well loved by the people of Edinburgh as to have been presented with a silver salver and 200 sovereigns raised by public subscription. Born in St Mary's Wynd in the Canongate, Smith worked as a printer and, from 1869, as librarian of the Mechanics' Library. His output included humorous sketches and nursery verse.

SYDNEY GOODSIR SMITH (1915–1975) was born in New Zealand, educated in England, and studied at Edinburgh and Oxford Universities. His interest in medieval Scots led him to adopt the language for his own work; his long love poem in Scots, *Under the Eildon Tree*, shows his mastery of the language; *Kynd Kittock's Land* too uses his brand of Scots to great effect in this piece set in the Royal Mile. His play *The Wallace* was performed at the Edinburgh Festival of 1960; and his poetry is gathered in *Collected Poems 1941–1975* (John Calder, 1975).

MURIEL SPARK (1918–2006) Born in Edinburgh, Muriel Spark was educated at James Gillespie's High School for Girls – undoubtedly the source of inspiration for her novel *The Prime of Miss Jean Brodie* – where she received the Walter Scott prize for poetry. Her first book was poetry (*The Fanfarlo and Other Verse*, 1952), and she always considered herself a poet, though finding greatest fame through her novels. Her life was not spent in Edinburgh and her attitude to the city was perhaps ambivalent. In 1993 she was made a Dame of the British Empire and in 2004 she visited the Edinburgh Book Festival and received the first ever Enlightenment Award. *All the Poems* (Carcanet) appeared in 2004.

LEWIS SPENCE (1874–1955) The author of many glittering words on Edinburgh, Spence was not a native of the city, but came to it as a student, having been born in Broughty Ferry. He worked as a journalist on *The Scotsman* and became an authority on ancient folklore and mythology, publishing widely in the field. With Hugh MacDiarmid, Spence was involved in the literary renaissance in Scotland in the 1920s, choosing to write in a version of Scots reminiscent of the sixteenth-century makars in *The Phoenix* (1923) and *Weirds and Vanities* (1927). Also like MacDiarmid, he was a nationalist, having been a founder member of the National Party of Scotland in 1928.

ROBERT LOUIS STEVENSON (1850–1894), author of the well-loved tales *Treasure Island* and *Kidnapped*, was also a poet. His best-known collection is *A Child's Garden of Verses*, but he also wrote lyric poetry and a range of lively verse in Scots. It was in his poetry that Stevenson most effectively expressed the pain of his separation from Scotland and from Edinburgh, the city of his birth. He travelled a lot, in search of a climate better suited to his poor health; he lived and died abroad, and is buried in Samoa. The most recent full edition of his poetry is *The Collected Poetry of Robert Louis Stevenson*, edited by Roger C. Lewis (Edinburgh University Press, 2003).

RUTHVEN TODD (1914–1978) Born in Edinburgh, Todd was educated at Fettes College and Edinburgh College of Art. He worked as a farm labourer on Mull, and then in Edinburgh, London, and the USA as a journalist and publisher, but is best known as a poet and writer of children's books. He left Scotland in 1931, but the poetry that returns to his Scottish roots is considered to be his most straightforward and best.

GAEL TURNBULL (1928–2004) was a medical practitioner in Britain, America and Canada, and returned to live in Edinburgh, where he was born. His work ranged from prose poetry and collage poems to his inventive "poem-objects"; all express a "delight in language and in the possibilities of utterance". He certainly delighted in taking to the streets with his kinetic poems during the Edinburgh Festival. His published poetry is collected in *There Are Words: Collected Poems* (Shearsman, 2006).

JOHN WHITWORTH (b.1945) Whitworth was removed to Edinburgh from an English childhood in 1955; the poems in *Landscape with Small Humans* (Peterloo, 1993) tell of culture shock, and schooldays in the city. He now lives in England. He edited *The Faber Book of Blue Verse* in 1990; his eighth collection, *The Whitworth Gun*, was published in 2002.

JAYNE WILDING was born in England, and moved to Scotland when she was six. She came to the University of Edinburgh at the age of seventeen and stayed until 2004, working as a freelance researcher and writer. She has taught creative writing for organisations like Artlink and Survivors' Poetry Scotland, and has been involved with Renga Platform events. Her book *In the Moon's Pantry* was published by diehard in 2005.

ACKNOWLEDGEMENTS

Our thanks are due to the following authors, publishers, and estates who have generously given permission to reproduce works:

Meg Bateman, "Gàrradh Moray Place, an Dùn Eideann / Moray Place Gardens, Edinburgh", from *Aotromachd agus dàin eile / Lightness and other poems* (Polygon, 1997), reprinted by permission of Polygon; **Norman Bissett**, an extract from "Angel of Morningside", first published in *Stand*, New Series Vol.2, no.3, September 2000, reprinted by permission of the author; **George Bruce**, "The Song of Henry Cockburn" from *Today Tomorrow: The Collected Poems of George Bruce 1933–2000* (Polygon, 2001), reprinted by permission of the George Bruce estate; **Ron Butlin**, "Edinburgh: A Place of my Own" from *Without a Backward Glance: New and Selected Poems* (Barzan, 2005), reprinted by permission of the author; **Angus Calder**, "Fin de Festival: Edinburgh 2000" from *Sun Behind the Castle: Edinburgh Poems* (Luath, 2004), reprinted by permission of Luath Press; **Stewart Conn**, "Choral Symphony" from *In the Kibble Palace: New and Selected Poems* (Bloodaxe, 1987), reprinted by permission of the author; "Close Names" from *Ghosts at Cockcrow* (Bloodaxe, 2005) and "From Arthur's Seat" from *Luncheon of the Boating Party* (Bloodaxe, 1992), reprinted by permission of Bloodaxe Books, www.bloodaxebooks.com; **Christine De Luca**, "Edinburgh Volte-face" from *Voes & Sounds* (Shetland Library, 1995), reprinted by permission of the author; **Douglas Fraser**, "Envoi" and "The Seat o' Inspiration" from *Rhymes o' Auld Reekie* (Macdonald, 1973), reprinted by permission of Heather Moncur; **Robert Garioch**, "At Robert Fergusson's Grave"; extract from "Embro to the Ploy" and "Nemo Canem Impune Lacessit" from *Collected Poems* (Polygon, 2004), reprinted by permission of Polygon; **Valerie Gillies**, "Edinburgh Under Snow" from *Bed of Stone* (Canongate, 1984), first published in Great Britain by Canongate Books Ltd, 14 High Street, Edinburgh EH1 1TE, reprinted by permission of Canongate Books Ltd; **George Campbell Hay**, "Edinburgh", and "Na Faoileagan Maidne / The Morning Gulls" from *Collected Poems and Songs* (Edinburgh University Press, 2000), reprinted by permission of the heirs of George Campbell Hay and the trustees of the W. L. Lorimer Trust Fund; **Hamish Henderson**, extract from "Floret Silva Undique" from *Collected Poems and Songs* (Curly Snake Publishing, 2000), reprinted by permission of Felicity Henderson; **Alexander Hutchison**, "Annals of Enlightenment" from *Makars' Walk* (Scottish Poetry Library / Edinburgh Old Town Trust, 1990), reprinted by permission of the author; **Liz Lochhead**, "Festival City: Yon Time Again" from *True Confessions* (Polygon, 2003), reprinted by permission of Polygon; **Brian McCabe**, "Buddha" from *Body Parts* (Canongate, 1999), first published in Great Britain by Canongate Books Ltd, 14 High Street, Edinburgh EH1 1TE, reprinted by permission of Canongate Books Ltd; **Norman MacCaig**, extract from "Double Life"; "Edinburgh Courtyard in July"; "November Night, Edinburgh" and "Old Edinburgh" from *The Poems of Norman MacCaig* (Polygon, 2005), reprinted by permission of Polygon; **Hugh MacDiarmid**, "Edinburgh", from *Complete Poems* Vol.II (Carcanet, 1994), reprinted by permission of Carcanet Press; **Stuart MacGregor**, "Northsong" from *Four Points of a Saltire* (Reprographia, 1970), reprinted by permission of Jane MacGregor; **Duncan Ban MacIntyre**, "Song of Edinburgh" from *Orain Dhonnchaidh Bhain / The Songs of Duncan Ban MacIntyre* (Scottish Gaelic Texts Society, 1952 and 1978), reprinted by permission of the Scottish Gaelic Texts Society; **Angela McSeveney**, "Edinburgh Suburb" and "Haiku" from *Coming Out With It* (Polygon, 1992), reprinted by permission of Polygon; **Gerald Mangan**, "Edinburgh" from *Waiting for the Storm* (Bloodaxe, 1990), reprinted by permission of the author; **Will H. Ogilvie**, "In Pentland Wine", reprinted by permission of Catherine Reid; **John W. Oliver**, "Peevers in Parliament Square" from *Peevers in*

Parliament Square (1975), reprinted by permission of Fraser Oliver; **Tessa Ransford**, "The City We Live In" from *A Dancing Innocence* (Macdonald, 1988), reprinted by permission of the author; **James Robertson**, "The Vision of Enric Miralles (1)" from *Voyage of Intent* (strangefruit, 2005), reprinted by permission of the author; **Robin Robertson**, "Dumb Show, with Candles", from the poem sequence "Camera Obscura" in *A Painted Field* (Picador, 1997), reprinted by permission of Pan Macmillan; **Iain Crichton Smith**, "Jean Brodie's Children" from *Collected Poems* (Carcanet, 1992), reprinted by permission of Carcanet Press; **Muriel Spark**, "Litany of Time Past" from *All the Poems* (Carcanet, 2004), reprinted by permission of David Higham Associates; **Ruthven Todd**, "In Edinburgh 1940" from *Garland for the Winter Solstice* (J. M. Dent & Sons, 1961), reprinted by permission of David Higham Associates Ltd; **Gael Turnbull**, extract from "The Edinburgh Poem", reprinted by permission of Jill Turnbull; **John Whitworth**, for "The Big School" from *Landscape with Small Humans* (Peterloo, 1993), reprinted by permission of Peterloo Poets; **Jayne Wilding**, for "On the Mend" from *In the Moon's Pantry* (diehard, 2004), reprinted by permission of the author. The editor and publishers would also like to thank Alice Bold for the lines quoted from Alan Bold's poem "Edinburgh".